THE MASTER'S VOICE

A Practical Guide to Personal Ministry

Ira L. Milligan

THE MASTER'S VOICE
A Practical Guide to Personal Ministry

By Ira L. Milligan
Copyright @ 2011 ShadeTree Publishing, LLC
1038 N. Eisenhower Dr. #274
Beckley, West Virginia 25801
ISBN 978-1-937331-06-1
Cover design by Christos Georghiou

All references to Greek word definitions are from Strong's Exhaustive Concordance, Thomas Nelson Publishers, 1990.

English word definitions are from The American Heritage Dictionary of the English Language, Third Edition, 1996, Houghton Mifflin Co.

All Scripture references are from the King James Version of the Bible, unless otherwise indicated. The King James Version is public domain in the United States.

Scriptures marked NKJ are taken from the New King James Version. Copyright 1979, 1980, 1982 by Thomas Nelson, Inc. Used by permission. All rights reserved.

All rights reserved. This book is protected by copyright. No part of this book may be reproduced or transmitted in any form or by any means, electronic or mechanical, including photocopying, recording, or by any information storage and retrieval system, without permission in writing from the publisher.

The purpose of this book is to educate and enlighten. This book is sold with the understanding that the author and publisher are not engaged in rendering counseling, albeit it professional or lay, to the reader or anyone else. The author and publisher shall have neither liability nor responsibility to any person or entity with respect to any loss or damage caused, or alleged to have been caused, directly or indirectly, by the information contained in this book. The information in this book does not necessarily reflect the opinion of the publisher.

The author has chosen to modernize the spelling of select words in Scripture to increase readability. *Italics* are used throughout for clarity of expression and for emphasis. They are sometimes used when quoting Scriptures for the same reason. The word *Church* is capitalized when it refers to the universal Church, including the whole Body of Christ. When referring to a local body of believers it is left un-capitalized. Similarly, the *Kingdom of God* is capitalized, but man's kingdom is not.

Visit our Web site at www.ShadeTreePublishing.com

For information about having a seminar conducted in your church, contact Ira at PO Box 1120 Tioga, LA. 71477.
Visit his website at www.Servant-Ministries.org.

DEDICATION

This book is dedicated to God's pioneers, the prophets. These men and women work on the very cutting edge of change. At times their lives may be hard and somewhat stressful, but seldom dull. May the Master richly reward their labors, bless their families for their continual sacrifices, and reserve a *special* place in heaven for them. They deserve it!

APPRECIATION

I wish to express my heartfelt thanks to those precious saints of God who have supported us with their prayers and substance to allow us to give ourselves wholly to prayer and to the ministry of the Word. A special thanks goes to my wife Judy, and my friends Jimmy, Mike, Matha, and Vicki for proof reading the manuscript and for their many helpful suggestions. Their wise counsel has made this a better book.

Contents

Introduction	1
Chapter One **Prophets, Then and Now**	3
Chapter Two **Let Jesus Testify**	9
Chapter Three **The Gift and the Office**	19
Chapter Four **Stop, Look, and Listen**	29
Chapter Five **The Reproof of Instruction**	39
Chapter Six **Submit Your Ministry**	53
Chapter Seven **Times and Seasons**	63
Chapter Eight **Prophets of Doom and Gloom**	69
Chapter Nine **Prophets, True and False**	75
Chapter Ten **Judging Prophecy**	83
Chapter Eleven **Elijah and Elisha**	89
Chapter Twelve **Prophetic Dreams and Visions**	95
Chapter Thirteen **His Potential in You**	101
Chapter Fourteen **Walking on His Word**	107
Chapter Fifteen **The Trial of Your Faith**	111
Chapter Sixteen **Clean Vessels and Pure Words**	119
Chapter Seventeen **Healing and Deliverance**	125
Chapter Eighteen **Unusual Manifestations**	133
Chapter Nineteen **Questions and Answers**	143
Seven Directives for Ministering the Gifts of the Spirit	157
About the Author	159

Introduction

Someone once said, "Experience is the best teacher," and as long as it's someone else's experience, it is! Regardless of how difficult the field, a few pioneers have to go first, and then be willing to share what they've learned before others can benefit from their sacrifice. That's the reason I've written this book. If it had been available about thirty years ago, it would have saved me a lot of grief.

We were young then, just getting started. We had the daunting task of *being* prophets, even though everyone thought prophets no longer existed. Things were a lot different than they are now, and harder. Not only were modern day prophets unheard of, when they were first introduced, they weren't too welcome, either. But we endured, and now there is wide acceptance of the prophetic ministry.

One reason things were hard then is there were few ministers teaching on the gifts of the spirit. Of necessity, everything we learned was by trial and error. Another reason things were difficult was there were almost no books written on this subject. In fact, when we first began ministering prophetically, there weren't *any* books on this subject at all – none that I knew of, at least. And even though there are several available now, none that I'm aware of gives you the close up, personal touch that this one does.

Although some ministries changed dramatically in the transition from Old Testament law to New Testament grace, the prophetic ministry remained virtually unchanged. *Thus saith the Lord* still carries with it the full and absolute authority of the King of kings, and Lord of lords. That's the reason it's important to get it right from the beginning.

No Christian should undertake ministering in Christ's stead without first learning to accurately represent Him in both word and spirit. "Word" alone is not enough, regardless of how accurate that word is.

When the time came for Jesus to go up to Jerusalem to be crucified, He attempted to pass through Samaria, but the Samaritans rejected Him and wouldn't allow Him through. James and John responded by asking Jesus whether they should, "command fire to come down from heaven, and consume them, even as Elijah did?" They had chapter and verse to support their request, but instead of granting them permission, Jesus "rebuked them, and said, Ye know not what manner of spirit ye are of" (Luke 9:54-56). Although they knew the Word of God quite well, they knew little about the God of the Word. They had read His book, and even knew the author, but they didn't understand Him yet. They still had a lot to learn.

Some things are *only* learned from personal experience – Christ's "manner of spirit" is one such thing – but it helps to have a few hints along the way.

This book is written to share over thirty years of prophetic experience with the reader. My prayer is that Christ will use it to save you from some of the bumps and bruises that we endured in learning these precepts, and perhaps use you to increase the precious flow of His prophetic word to His dry and thirsty people. *Enjoy!*

CHAPTER ONE
Prophets, Then and Now

> Surely the Lord God does nothing, Unless He reveals His secret to His servants the prophets
> -Amos 3:7, NKJ

The first time I heard anyone called a prophet was in Oklahoma City, Oklahoma, in early 1972. I, along with two other ministers, was visiting a Pentecostal church the like of which I'd never experienced before. During worship, in lulls between songs, young children stood up and told visions they saw while worshiping. The pastor patiently interpreted each one as it was described.

At another point in the service, a young man stood and walked about prophesying various encouraging words to the congregation. It was obvious that what we were observing was perfectly normal "church" to everyone there, except us! Toward the end of the service a woman carrying a tape recorder and "pastor Ed" approached me with "a word from the Lord." What transpired next nearly blew me away!

"Prophet; Prophet; Thou has heard My voice and fear has struck thine heart; Thou has even tried to hide away, but I say unto thee that you cannot hide from ME, THE SPIRIT OF THE LORD," pastor Ed's voice rose strongly, booming forth in distinct, old King James English, "I loose the spirit of a prophet that it might come forth; For this day a true word shall be spoken unto My people; I have laid it upon thee as a fire upon thee, that thou would speak the word of the Lord, with assurance and with authority...," he continued. Then he began to speak of things that only

I, and the two men with me, knew. We listened in stunned silence.

I was so amazed that at first I wondered whether he were actually speaking to someone else instead of me. Up until that moment, I had not even *thought* about the possibility of anyone being a prophet in this day and time, much less considered myself as one! I left that service with his words buzzing in my head.

Although I had been introduced to the gift of prophecy several years before, I had not experienced it to that depth and accuracy, and I certainly hadn't considered myself a prophet. But God was about to change all that, although it would be several more years before I would fully understand what it was all about. I still had much to learn about prophets and the gift of prophecy.

The First Outpouring

> And it shall come to pass in the last days, saith God, I will pour out of my Spirit upon all flesh: *and your sons and your daughters shall prophesy,* and your young men shall see visions, and your old men shall dream dreams: And on my servants and on my handmaidens I will pour out... my Spirit; *and they shall prophesy.*
> —Acts 2:17-18, italics mine

Most Christians are aware that in Acts, chapter 2, God promised to pour out the spirit of prophecy upon His people in the last days, but the first example of a public outpouring is actually found in Numbers 11:16-17. In this passage, Moses cried out to God in his frustration with Israel as he led them through the wilderness. Their continual murmuring and complaining was just too much for him to bear. God responded to Moses' cries for help by commanding him to gather seventy men from among Israel's many elders, promising him that He would come down and talk with them.

> And I will come down and talk with thee there: and I will take of the spirit which is upon thee, and will put it upon them; and *they shall bear the burden of the people with thee,* that thou bear it not thyself alone
> —Numbers 11:17; italics mine

The express purpose of this ordination was to enable these men to, "bear the burden of the people" with Moses. When Moses' prophetic anointing came upon the seventy, "they prophesied, and did not cease" (Numbers 11:25).

Their newly found gifts stirred up envy then, just as they do now. Moses' servant Joshua heard two of them prophesying in the camp and came running to Moses, crying: "My lord Moses, forbid them." Moses' reply revealed his heart then, and Christ's heart now.

> And Moses said unto him, Enviest thou for my sake? *would God that all the Lord's people were prophets*, and that the Lord would put his spirit upon them!
> —Numbers 11:28-29, italics mine

Prophets Today

God still wants His people to be prophets. Why shouldn't He? Prophets are trained to *listen*. As a result, they speak His word and do His will like no other.

Although some of the other ministries may have changed in the transition from Old Testament law to

THE MASTER'S VOICE

New Testament grace, the prophetic anointing and purpose remains virtually unchanged. The spiritual shepherds of Israel first served as judges, and later ruled as kings, while the Church's shepherds serve as pastors and elders.

The Old Testament deliverers led armies into bloody battles while wielding swords and shields, whereas New Testament apostles' directed armies of intercessors into spiritual warfare armed only with the Spirit and Word of God. But, with few exceptions, prophets still use the same weapons they've always used. Their ministry hasn't changed, and their purpose remains the same.

Prophets directed and encouraged God's armies then, and when and where they are recognized and accepted, they still do today. They counseled and challenged natural kings who ruled over the world's kingdoms then, and today they counsel and challenge the spiritual leaders of the greatest Kingdom of all, the Kingdom of Heaven. *Thus saith the Lord* still carries with it the full and absolute authority of the King of kings and Lord of lords. That will never change.

The prophetic anointing is one of the most valuable allies a leader can have, whether he is in civil or ecclesiastical government. If the leader doesn't personally have the prophetic anointing, he needs someone who will work closely with him who does. The gift of prophecy is a leader's eyes and ears. Without it, the blind will lead the blind.

The Gentile church of Antioch gives us an excellent model for good, balanced, church government. Today, most modern churches readily recognize the ministry of *pastor*-teachers, but Antioch's leadership team consisted of five *prophet*-teachers. What's the difference? Pastor-teachers are trained to minister the written word. Prophet-teachers are trained to minister the word *and* the Spirit.

> Now there were in the church that was at Antioch certain *prophets* and *teachers*; as Barnabas, and Simeon that was called Niger, and Lucius of Cyrene, and Manaen... and Saul
> -Acts 13:1; italics mine

The Jerusalem church also had its share of prophet-teachers. Two were sent to Antioch with Paul and Barnabas to confirm their message of grace to the Gentile churches.

> Then pleased it the apostles and elders, with the whole church, to send chosen men of their own company to Antioch with Paul and Barnabas; namely, *Judas... and Silas, chief men among the brethren...* And Judas and Silas, *being prophets also themselves, exhorted the brethren* with many words, *and confirmed them.*
> -Acts 15:22, 32; italics mine

After their mission was complete, Judas returned to Jerusalem, but Silas stayed in Antioch and later joined Paul's apostolic team and traveled on the mission field with him (see Acts 15:32-41).

As the time for Christ's return grows ever nearer, the Church's need for apostolic and prophetic ministry teams grows clearer. The support ministry provided by the prophets is indispensable. There is no substitute. The church needs more than just pastors and teachers. The spiritual ministry supplied by the prophetic anointing must be restored to the Church. God must once again raise up prophets to strengthen and confirm the brethren in preparation for His coming.

THE MASTER'S VOICE

> Follow after charity, and desire spiritual gifts, but rather that ye may prophesy... [for] he that prophesies speaks unto men to edification, and exhortation, and comfort
>
> -1 Corinthians 14:1,3

Chapter Two
Let Jesus Testify

> The testimony of the Lord is sure, making wise the simple
>
> -Psalm 19:7

When John wrote, "the testimony of Jesus is the spirit of prophecy" (Revelation 19:10), he gave us an important key toward unlocking the mysteries of the prophetic gifts. Jesus is eternal, immortal, ruling with absolute power and authority, but it wasn't always that way. When He first came in mortal flesh, He was the same as all other men, weak and subject to temptation. Through the Holy Spirit's power and guidance, which the Father freely gave to Him at His baptism, He overcame everything Satan had to throw at Him.

Christ was rejected by His own people, tempted with all the sinful pleasures the world had to offer, afflicted, mocked, tormented and finally, crucified. He was falsely accused, tried and executed like a common thief; yet, He died without sin. But then, after three days, He *arose*. That is Christ's testimony. Sin couldn't enslave Him; death couldn't defeat Him; and the grave couldn't hold Him. He arose to live and reign forever, "after the power of an endless life" (Hebrews 7:16).

After His resurrection, Jesus appeared before John and gave His personal testimony.

> I am he that lives, and was dead; and, behold, I am alive for evermore, Amen; and have the keys of hell and of death
>
> -Revelation 1:18

His testimony declares that He has absolute supremacy. When He arose, He sat down at His Father's right hand, "Far above all principality, and power, and might, and dominion, and every name that is named, not only in this world, but also in that which is to come" (Ephesians 1:21). Through the power of His resurrection, He now reigns with total, unlimited authority over all things – both visible and invisible – things in heaven and things on earth. He is King of kings, Lord of lords, and God of gods. He reigns victoriously over death, hell and the grave, Such is the *spirit* of prophecy!

Jesus said, "We speak what We know and testify what We have seen" (John 3:11; NKJ). Christ experienced suffering, torture and death – and then, resurrection power. He knows what life and death are all about. He understands exactly what we're going through, "For we have not an high priest which cannot be touched with the feeling of our infirmities; but was in all points tempted like as we are, yet without sin" (Hebrews 4:15). When Christ speaks through the spirit of prophecy, He speaks with compassion and concern. He knows from personal experience exactly how we feel.

The Best Gift

His testimony releases resurrection power, for Christ didn't just endure problems like ours, He solved them. He vanquished our foes and ascended on high, pouring out gifts unto men. His gifts release power. *Prophecy releases resurrection power.* Who wouldn't want a gift like that?

That's the reason Paul admonished his converts to seek for the gift of prophecy, which he clearly revealed is the best gift of all (see 1 Corinthians 12:31; 14:1, 39). Although anyone who is filled with the Holy Spirit has the potential to prophesy, and the Scriptures clearly give all Christians permission to prophesy, before anyone *can* prophesy he or she must receive the gift of prophecy. Ask for it; seek for it; knock until you receive it. Like all of God's gifts, prophecy is free. The only qualification necessary to receive it is faith. One must believe to receive.

Dead Men Don't Talk

Although today, many believe that the gifts of the spirit no longer exist, and indeed, in some churches they don't, that's certainly not what God intended. Paul wrote to the Corinthians:

> That in every thing ye are enriched by him, in all utterance, and in all knowledge; even as *the testimony of Christ was confirmed in you: So that ye come behind in no gift;* waiting for the coming of our Lord Jesus Christ: *Who shall also confirm you unto the end,* that ye may be blameless in the day of our Lord Jesus Christ
> -1 Corinthians 1:5-8, italics mine

Since the end isn't here, the gifts haven't ceased. Christ is still testifying. Dead men don't talk – live men do! Jesus is alive, and through His gifts, He is still testifying of His resurrection. In fact, Paul said that when the church allows Jesus to freely testify, an unbelieving, visiting sinner's reaction will be "falling down on his face he will worship God, and report that God is in you of a truth" (1 Corinthians 14:25). The modern Church could use a report like that!

Cessationist Theology

In light of all the negative publicity the Church has endured through the national media these last few decades, it could certainly use a news report, which declares, "God is in you of a truth," but it doesn't have one. Why? Because in many cases, God isn't in it.

By teaching that the day of miracles is past, liberal theologians effectively deny the resurrection. Their doctrine, called *cessationist theology*, teaches that all supernatural gifts and manifestations "ceased" with the passing of the twelve apostles and the writing of the Scriptures. By ignoring the plain teaching of Scripture and denying the Spirit's power, these theologians make the same error the Sadducees of Jesus' day made. Jesus told them, "Ye do err, not knowing the scriptures, nor the power of God" (Matthew 22:29).

New Testament Prophecy

One of their objections is that the Scriptures don't contain any New Testament examples of personal prophecy. But, this objection is faulty because it simply isn't true. While Jesus was still an infant, both He and His mother were given a personal prophecy in the temple at His dedication.

> And Simeon blessed them, and said unto Mary his mother, Behold, this child is set for the fall and rising again of many in Israel; and for a sign which shall be spoken against (Yea, a sword shall pierce through thy own soul also,) that the thoughts of many hearts may be revealed
> -Luke 2:34-35

After this prophecy was fulfilled in Christ's crucifixion and resurrection from the grave, Jesus gave Peter a personal word which foretold the conditions which would surround Peter's death.

> Most assuredly, I say to you, when you were younger, you girded yourself and walked where you wished; but when you are old, you will stretch out your hands, and another will gird you and carry you where you do not wish. This He spoke, signifying by what death he would glorify God
> -John 21:18-19; NKJ

Although Peter was spared Herod's attempts on his life when he was young, just like Jesus' prophecy predicted, history records that when he was old he was bound and crucified. In fact, Peter even mentioned Christ's personal word to him right before he was martyred (see Acts 12:1-17; 2 Peter 1:14).

Another example of personal prophecy occurred immediately after Paul's first encounter with Christ on the road to Damascus. The Lord appeared to a man named Ananias and told him to go minister to Paul, telling him that Paul was, "a chosen vessel unto me, to bear my name before the Gentiles, and kings, and the children of Israel: For I will show him how great things he must suffer for my name's sake" (Acts 9:15-16).

Years later, as Paul was returning to Jerusalem from his third missionary journey, he received another similar prophecy. God's message hadn't changed much, only this time it was more specific.

THE MASTER'S VOICE

> And when [Agabus] was come unto us, he took Paul's girdle, and bound his own hands and feet, and said, Thus saith the Holy Ghost, So shall the Jews at Jerusalem bind the man that owns this girdle, and shall deliver him into the hands of the Gentiles
>
> -Acts 21:11

This wasn't the first time Paul had heard this. In fact, personal prophecy was so common in the early Church that everywhere Paul went, he heard the same thing. He said, "the Holy Ghost witnesses in every city, saying that bonds and afflictions abide me" (Acts 20:23).

Paul not only *received* warnings through prophecy, he ministered a few himself. In fact, one in particular was rather dramatic. On Paul's first missionary journey, he encountered a sorcerer named Bar-Jesus, who foolishly tried to stop him from ministering to the deputy of Paphos.

> Then Saul, (who also is called Paul,) filled with the Holy Ghost, set his eyes on him, And said, O full of all subtlety and all mischief, thou child of the devil, thou enemy of all righteousness, wilt thou not cease to pervert the right ways of the Lord? And now, behold, the hand of the Lord is upon thee, and thou shalt be blind, not seeing the sun for a season. And immediately there fell on him a mist and a darkness; and he went about seeking some to lead him by the hand
>
> -Acts 13:9-11

Another prophetic warning Paul gave was when he made his last trip to Jerusalem. He summoned the elders from Ephesus to meet him in Miletus, and there correctly predicted they would never see his face again. Then he warned them that after his departing "grievous wolves [shall] enter in among you, not sparing the flock. Also of your own selves shall men arise, speaking perverse things, to draw away disciples after them" (Acts 20:25,29-30).

The elders must have taken his warning seriously because a few years later John wrote a letter to the Ephesians and commended them because they had successfully, "tried them which say they are apostles, and are not, and hast found them liars" (Revelation 2:2).

Soon after Paul's arrival in Jerusalem, as Agabus had prophesied, Paul was bound in chains and sent by ship to Rome. After only a few days of sailing, Paul prophesied to the centurion who had charge over him that disaster lay ahead, but his words fell on deaf ears.

> And [Paul] said unto them, Sirs, I perceive that this voyage will be with hurt and much damage, not only of the lading and ship, but also of our lives. Nevertheless the centurion believed the master and the owner of the ship, more than those things which were spoken by Paul
> -Acts 27:10-11

A few weeks later the ship was completely destroyed by a violent typhoon named *Euroclydon*, but God mercifully spared everyone aboard.

Public Prophecy

Public prophecies to the individual congregations were common then, too. Luke gives us one example:

> And in these days came prophets from Jerusalem unto Antioch. And there stood up one of them

named Agabus, and signified by the spirit that there should be great dearth throughout all the world: which came to pass in the days of Claudius Caesar.
-Acts 11:27-28

John gave us several more examples in his letters to the seven churches of Asia (see Revelation Chapters 2 and 3).

The Fear of Man

There is no question about it, the modern, liberal theologians are wrong. The Scriptures clearly show that both personal and congregational prophecy was ordinary in the early Church, and there is *no* scriptural justification for teaching that it's not for today. In fact, in Acts 2:17, God promised to pour out His Spirit in these last days and both His sons and daughters *would* prophesy!

Why, then, isn't prophecy a common practice in the Church today? Besides the unbelief generated by cessationist theology, what is the main reason more Christians aren't prophesying in the churches now?

Undoubtedly, the answer is fear – and not just any fear – but the fear of man. The Bible says, "The fear of man brings a snare" (Proverbs 29:25). Like a trap set to catch and hold animals, fear snares men, holding them back and preventing them from obeying the Holy Spirit. Sometimes even God's simplest admonitions are beyond their reach.

Stage fright is one example of this type of fear, but the fear of man goes beyond public speaking. Many Christians are even afraid to witness one-on-one. The same holds true when they are called upon to prophesy, whether publicly or privately. For many, fear rules instead of God's Spirit. One cannot yield to the fear of rejection from others and still obtain God's full approval.

When Christians no longer fear what others think of them, they can hear God clearly enough to speak for Him. Jesus said:

> As I hear, I judge: and my judgment is just; *because I seek not mine own will, but the will of the Father* which hath sent me.
> -John 5:30b, italics mine

Our *will* constantly influences what we hear, either opening our ears to hear the still small voice of God, or closing them completely, where even the loudest trumpet cannot be heard. In other words, we hear what we want to hear.

Jesus asked the Jews, "How can ye believe, which receive honor one of another, and seek not the honor that comes from God only?" (John 5:44). As Christians, we have two options. We can either have God's honor or man's, but not both. Paul said, "do I seek to please men? For if I yet pleased men, I should not be the servant of Christ" (Galatians 1:10). Fear of losing the honor of their peers keeps many from hearing, and faith comes by hearing, so those who cannot hear remain in unbelief.

Obviously, Timothy suffered this malady. Paul placed him in charge of the work in Ephesus while Timothy was still a young man. After Paul left, he wrote back to him, cautioning Timothy not to allow himself to be intimidated by the older members of his congregation (see 1 Timothy 4:12). Later, in Paul's second letter, he urged him to stir up his prophetic gift.

THE MASTER'S VOICE

> Wherefore I put thee in remembrance that thou stir up the gift of God, which is in thee by the putting on of my hands. For God hath not given us the spirit of fear; but of power, and of love, and of a sound mind. Be not thou therefore ashamed of the testimony of our Lord.
>
> -2 Timothy 1:6-8

Although Paul had imparted the gift of prophecy to Timothy through the laying on of hands, his gift lay dormant because Timothy was afraid that if he attempted to prophesy and "missed it," he would be embarrassed by his failure. So, he opted not to prophesy at all. Paul gently reminded him that his fear of failure wasn't from his Savior, but from his enemy.

Yielding to fear and not prophesying is the greatest failure of all. Christ longs to testify through every one of us, and His testimony is invaluable. It is a powerful, irrefutable witness of His resurrection.

> He that hath received his testimony hath set to his seal that God is true.
>
> -John 3:33

CHAPTER THREE
The Gift and the Office

> For as we have many members in one body, and all members have not the same office.
> -Romans 12:4

As Moses led the children of Israel around in circles in the desert, they became increasingly difficult to deal with. The longer they walked, the more they murmured and complained. In his frustration with them, Moses cried out to God for help. God responded by pouring out His Spirit upon seventy of Israel's elders, and so they started prophesying. When this happened Joshua came running to Moses asking him to make them stop. Moses refused. Instead, he replied:

> Enviest thou for my sake? Would God that all the Lord's people were prophets, and that the Lord would put his spirit upon them!
> -Numbers 11:29

Paul must have agreed with Moses, at least in part, because he told us what would happen if all the saints did prophesy.

> But if all prophesy, and there come in one that believeth not, or one unlearned, he is convinced of all, he is judged of all.
> -1 Corinthians 14:24

But, after Paul listed the Church's various offices and ministries, he asked, "Are all apostles? Are all prophets?" with the implied answer of "No, of course they're not."

> God has set some in the church, first apostles, secondarily prophets, thirdly teachers, after that miracles, then gifts of healings, helps, governments, diversities of tongues. Are all apostles? *are all prophets?* are all teachers? are all workers of miracles?
> -1 Corinthians 12:28-29, italics mine

So, if all can have the gift of prophecy and prophesy, yet all who prophesy are not prophets, what's the difference between the two? Although this issue is rather complex, there is one very simple explanation: one is a gift, the other is an office. A gift denotes ability; an office denotes responsibility.

The Gift of Prophecy

First, let's examine the gift. The gift of prophecy is one of the nine manifestations of the Spirit discussed in chapter twelve and fourteen of First Corinthians. Both gifted saints and prophets use this described anointing. Although the more familiar "gift of tongues" and "interpretation of tongues" is similar, they serve slightly different purposes. Both prophecy and the gift of tongues are divine utterances; both proclaim God's will. But Paul said the gift of tongues is for a sign, especially when it is used to give public oracles. The tongues are to convince unbelievers of the supernatural source of the message. On the other hand, believers should not require such proof, so according to Paul, when there are no unbelievers present, the tongues should be dispensed with and only the message itself given (see 1 Corinthians 14:22-24).

A true prophetic utterance will always conform to the righteous principles of God's written word. Prophecy is *one* of the ways He has chosen to reveal His will unto mankind. The gift of prophecy enables anyone who has it to give a divine oracle for God. Peter said:

> As every man hath received the gift, even so minister the same one to another, as good stewards of the manifold grace of God. If any man speak, let him speak as the oracles of God; if any man minister, let him do it as of the ability which God giveth: that God in all things may be glorified through Jesus Christ.
> -1 Peter 4:10-11a

Although every saint of God has the *privilege* of speaking for the Master, only those who have received the gift of prophecy have the *ability* to do so.

Many Are Called

Jesus said, "many are called, but few are chosen" (Matthew 22:14). God calls men, equips them for His service, trains them for His work, and then tests them to assure they are qualified and ready. Those who pass, He commissions to do His bidding. Many are called, but because only a few can (or will) endure the rigorous training and testing required, only a few are sent. Many fail and are rejected.

In the military, carrier pilots and Navy Seals undergo much harder and more strenuous training than ordinary airmen and foot soldiers. When student pilots and Seal candidates wash out and fail to make the grade, they aren't thrown out of the military, but transferred to other departments better suited to their temperaments and abilities. So it is in God's army.

Greater callings usually require longer and harder training programs and tougher tests. Sometimes God's boot camp can be brutal! Joseph, who was called to greatness to save both his people and the whole nation of Egypt from a devastating famine, was sold into slavery and spent most of his early years in prison. Moses spent forty years tending sheep on the back side of the desert before God sent him to deliver his nation. David suffered relentless persecution from King Saul before he was crowned king over Israel. And the greatest King of all had to endure rejection from His own people and suffer crucifixion at the hands of envious priests and cruel soldiers before being declared Lord of all.

Advancement in His Kingdom

My mother used to say, "If you want something done, give the job to someone who is already busy." That appears to be God's motto too. In one of Jesus' parables, He said a certain Nobleman turned his estate over to his servants and left to acquire a kingdom for himself. Upon returning, he called them in to give an account of their business transactions while he was gone (see Luke 19:12-27). The first servant proudly showed him the results of his trading, saying, "Lord, thy pound hath gained ten pounds" (Luke 19:16).

The Nobleman quickly rewarded his industrious servant by promoting him and giving him authority over ten cities in his newly acquired kingdom.

> And he said unto him, Well, thou good servant: because thou hast been faithful in a very little, have thou authority over ten cities.
> -Luke 19:17

Likewise, the Nobleman rewarded his second servant's diligence with a promotion over five cities. Each man's promotion was in direct proportion to his labors. But when the Nobleman confronted the last servant, all he had to offer for his tenure of service was a lame excuse. He even blamed his lord for his own failure!

> And another came, saying, *Lord, behold, here is thy pound, which I have kept laid up in a napkin: For I feared thee, because thou art an austere man:* thou takest up that thou layedst not down, and reapest that thou didst not sow. And he saith unto him... Wherefore then gavest not thou my money into the bank, that at my coming I might have required mine own with usury? And he said unto them that stood by, *Take from him the pound, and give it to him that hath ten pounds.* (And they said unto him, Lord, he hath ten pounds.) For I say unto you, That unto every one which hath shall be given; and from him that hath not, even that he hath shall be taken away from him.
> -Luke 19:20-26, italics mine

Use it or lose it. God's callings are by grace alone, but His rewards are directly proportional to your service. If you aren't a self-starter, then offer your gifts and services to your pastor (spiritual banker), and allow him to invest them for you. At least you won't lose out completely when He returns.

From Gifting to Office

> For promotion cometh neither from the east, nor from the west, nor from the south. But God is the judge: he puts down one, and sets up another.
> -Psalm 75:6-7

There are two different types of promotions in God's Kingdom. One is advancing from gifting to office, and the other is promotion from a lower office to a higher one. An example of advancing from gifting to office is Samson.

Judges 13:25 says "the Spirit of the Lord began to move him at times in the camp of Dan between Zorah and Eshtaol." During this time, God introduced Samson to a lion.

> Then went Samson down... to the vineyards of Timnath: and, behold, a young lion roared against him. And the Spirit of the Lord came mightily upon him, and he rent him as he would have rent a kid, and he had nothing in his hand.
> -Judges 14:5-6a

After this terrifying experience, Samson realized that he was gifted. Samson wasn't the smartest man in the world, but he knew full well that without God's anointing, he wasn't strong enough to kill a lion with his bare hands. So, his supernatural encounter convinced his heart, and his faith rose dramatically. Soon, God completed his training and gave him a promotion. The reigns were placed into his own hands.

Now, instead of God moving Samson, Samson moved God. This change corresponds to advancing from gifting (having divine ability) to office (having authority and responsibility). For example, many who faithfully use the gift of prophecy are later promoted to the office of prophet. Of those, some will receive further promotion into apostolic service.

As long as God holds the reigns, you aren't responsible to do anything other than obey. You can do only what He specifically moves you to do. When He turns the control over to you, you are responsible to stir up the gift and use it as occasion demands. As Samuel prophesied to Saul at his ordination, when God promoted him to the king's office:

> Then Samuel took a vial of oil, and poured it upon [Saul's] head, and kissed him, and said, Is it not because the Lord hath anointed thee to be captain over his inheritance?... And let it be, when these signs are come unto thee, that thou do as occasion serve thee; for God is with thee.
> -1 Samuel 10:1,7

Up until his promotion, Saul wasn't responsible for Israel's deliverance, but from that time on, he was.

From Office to Office

In the second type of advancement, where we are promoted from a lower office to a higher one, the higher office usually retains most of the duties of the lower, only additional authority and responsibilities are added. For example, Barnabas and Saul served faithfully as prophets and teachers before they were promoted to apostles.

> Now there were in the church that was at Antioch certain prophets and teachers; as Barnabas... and Saul. As they ministered to the Lord, and fasted, the Holy Ghost said, Separate me Barnabas and Saul for the work whereunto I have called them. And when they had fasted and prayed, and laid their hands on them, they sent them away. So

> they, being sent forth by the Holy Ghost, departed unto Seleucia; and from thence they sailed to Cyprus.
>
> -Acts 13:1-4

Once they were promoted and "sent forth," their job description changed dramatically. Before, they were partially responsible for one church. Afterward, they were fully responsible for many.

Ability vs Responsibility

Although true prophets normally have the gift of prophecy, they do far more than just prophesy. As we said in the beginning of this chapter, the primary difference between the two is ability versus responsibility. Prophets not only have the ability to speak accurately for God, but they are responsible to watch for the flock. God told Ezekiel:

> Son of man, I have made thee a watchman unto the house of Israel: therefore hear the word at my mouth, and give them warning from me.
>
> -Ezekiel 3:17

Since prophets are responsible to watch for the enemy, they have authority to warn the people when they see him coming. God chooses His own watchmen, so their authority is from Him, and they are accountable to Him.

When He sounds the warning, they must warn the people. If the saints heed their warnings, they're safe; if they don't, they not only have the enemy to deal with, they're also in trouble with God. Those who do not heed His watchmen will not be held guiltless. Likewise, those who resist His prophets and restrict or hinder them in their duties incur His anger. God said,

"Touch not mine anointed, and do my prophets no harm" (Psalm 105:15).

Persecution and Rejection

On the other hand, men and women who are prophets cannot always expect special protection or favors. Jesus said:

> Wherefore, behold, I send unto you prophets, and wise men, and scribes: and some of them ye shall kill and crucify; and some of them shall ye scourge in your synagogues, and persecute them from city to city.
> -Matthew 23:34

Special favors are only awarded after the job is done.

> Blessed are ye, when men shall revile you, and persecute you, and shall say all manner of evil against you falsely, for my sake. *Rejoice, and be exceeding glad: for great is your reward in heaven...*
> -Matthew 5:11-12, italics mine

THE MASTER'S VOICE

CHAPTER FOUR
Stop, Look, and Listen

> *But if all prophesy*, and there come in one that believeth not, or one unlearned, he is convinced of all, he is judged of all: And thus are the secrets of his heart made manifest; and so falling down on his face he will worship God, and report that God is in you of a truth. How is it then, brethren? when ye come together, *every one of you* hath a psalm, hath a doctrine, hath a tongue, hath a revelation, hath an interpretation. Let all things be done unto edifying... *For ye may all prophesy* one by one, that all may learn, and all may be comforted.
>
> -1 Corinthians 14:24-26, 31, italics mine

Who May Prophesy?

As we discussed in Chapter Three, every saint has the privilege of prophesying. Paul said, "ye may all prophesy." Through the universal priesthood of the believer, anyone who will stand in God's presence and hear His word can speak for Him. There is nothing but unbelief to prevent a Christian from prophesying. In the same way, a father will tell his young son to, "Go tell momma it's time to cook supper", our heavenly Father will send us to speak for Him, too. Spiritual age isn't a factor. Paul prayed for twelve new converts and every one of them immediately began prophesying.

> And when Paul had laid his hands upon [the twelve new believers], the Holy Ghost came on them; and they spake with tongues, *and prophesied*.
>
> -Acts 19:6, italics mine

Physical age isn't a factor either. God called Jeremiah into the prophetic ministry while he was still a small child. When he objected, the Lord responded: "Say not, I am a child: for thou shalt go to all that I shall send thee, and whatsoever I command thee thou shalt speak" (Jeremiah 1:7). After all, it's not the child's testimony that counts, it's Christ's. He's the one with something important to say!

Samuel was another who started prophesying in his youth (see 1 Samuel 3:8-10). It's a lot easier to teach children to prophesy than adults, because children are not as concerned about embarrassing themselves if they miss God. If they say something wrong, they just do as any baby learning to walk; they simply get up and try again.

A person's gender doesn't enter into the picture either. Peter said, "your sons *and your daughters* shall prophesy" (Acts 2:17, italics mine). In fact, all four of Phillip the evangelist's daughters prophesied (see Acts 21:8-9).

Spiritual Exercises

Although prophecy has two primary anointings, and many different dimensions, the actual act of prophesying is easy. In its simplest form prophesying is listening to what the Holy Spirit is saying and repeating it verbatim. When the word of knowledge and the word of wisdom are added, things get a little more complex (see 1 Corinthians 12:8). But regardless of how complex it gets, learning to prophesy accurately involves becoming sensitive to one's spiritual senses.

We have five natural senses and five spiritual senses. Hebrews 5:14 says that adults have, "their senses exercised to discern both good and evil." Almost any adult can walk into a dark room and find a light switch by feeling along a wall, avoid tripping over limbs on a wooded path by watching where he's going, recognize an approaching train by listening to its whistle blow, or discern whether meat is spoiled or fresh by tasting or smelling it. Yet, none of these acts are instinctive; they are all learned behavior.

As children we quickly learn what "hot" means when our mother cautions us at the stove. As we mature and become more experienced, we learn to recognize when a child has fever by feeling of his or her brow. Likewise, through experience, we soon learn to recognize when someone is displeased or angry with us by both what we see in their face and hear in their voice. Yet, many Christians live all their lives without realizing that God expects them to learn to exercise their spiritual senses, too.

Learning to Prophesy

Many Christians think that it is impossible to learn to do something supernatural, but nothing could be further from the truth. Paul said, "ye may all prophesy one by one, *that all may learn*" (1 Corinthians 14:31, italics mine). We learn to walk one step at a time. We learn to talk by listening and imitating what we hear. We learn to prophesy one step and one word at a time, too.

Those who stumble over the idea of *learning* to prophesy reason that if prophecy is a gift from God, then He's the One prophesying, not us. But, that's not the way spiritual gifts work. For instance, two manifestations of the supernatural gift of tongues are praying and giving messages. In Paul's teachings on how to use this gift, he said, "For if I pray in an unknown tongue, my spirit prayeth" (1 Corinthians 14:14a). Notice, he said *my* spirit is the one doing the praying, not the Holy Spirit. Praying in the spirit, giving messages in tongues, and prophesying are all the same. The Holy Spirit enables *our* spirit to pray and prophesy – He doesn't do it for us.

A spiritual gift can be compared to a natural talent. If children are gifted with musical talents, they can easily learn to play an instrument and sing. Nevertheless, regardless of how talented they may be, very few can achieve excellence without being trained. Likewise, if God's children are gifted to prophesy, they will excel only with proper training.

We have all heard the old adage: practice makes perfect. Excellence in ministry is acquired the same way, regardless of which gift is being exercised. Ministering properly requires gifting, training and experience, and neither of these is any more or less important than the other; all three are indispensable.

Stop, Look, and Listen

The easiest way to learn is by laying hands on people and praying for them. As you pray, stop, look, and listen. *Stop* controlling your own thoughts and allow the Holy Spirit to influence your prayers. As you pray, *look* to see if He is showing you something about the person you are praying for, and *listen* to what He is having you say as you pray.

By relaxing control and allowing the Holy Spirit to direct your prayers, you give Him an opportunity to reveal the secrets of that person's heart to you. Paul said that all of our prayers should be of this type.

> Praying always with all prayer and supplication in the Spirit, and watching thereunto with all perseverance and supplication for all saints.
> -Ephesians 6:18

Notice that Paul mentioned "watching" in the above passage. Part of watching in prayer is learning to see. God transmits pictures into our imagination in the same way that He imparts thoughts into our thinking processes. Although some of these "visions" are bright and vivid, many are not.

God will often paint fleeting, yet accurate visions upon the canvas of your imagination as you are praying and ministering. The trick is learning to acknowledge what you see.

God started training Jeremiah to prophesy while he was still a child. The way He taught Jeremiah is still the same way that He teaches us today. He showed him a limb from an almond tree and then asked him what he was seeing:

> Moreover the word of the Lord came unto me, saying, Jeremiah, what seest thou? And I said, I see a rod of an almond tree. Then said the Lord unto me, Thou hast well seen: for I will hasten my word to perform it.
> -Jeremiah 1:11-12

As soon as Jeremiah acknowledged what he saw, God told him what his vision meant.

Paul wrote to Philemon and told him, "the communication of thy faith may become effectual by the acknowledging of every good thing which is in you in Christ Jesus" (Philemon 1:6). When we acknowledge the thoughts and visions that the Holy Spirit gives us, we become effective in communicating our faith. As long as we keep questioning what we hear, and doubting what we see, we are ineffective because we are not ministering in faith.

Mental Hindrances

While you are attempting to minister, your own thoughts will often get in your way. Thoughts like, "That's not God, that's just my own imagination," are perfectly natural. However, if you believe them, they will rob you of the joy of ministering for the Lord. If you will learn to resist your negative thoughts and ask the people you are ministering to whether the "word" or "vision" that you've received relates to them, you will quickly learn the difference between your own thoughts and the Holy Spirit's. A very important part of this training process involves learning to feel.

Learning to Feel

With experience, you can discern whether a particular thought is from God or not through the sense of feel. Feeling enables you to recognize the anointing of prophecy; know when God is nudging you to speak, or not to speak; and while ministering, even know when you've used a word that doesn't accurately depict what the Spirit was trying to say. This allows you to stay on track and correct slight misconceptions or misunderstandings as you go.

Of all the senses we possess, feeling is undoubtedly the most important. It is certainly the one we use the most. In the natural, feeling is almost the only sense that we have that is useful in the dark. Blind people feed themselves, walk about without stumbling–even read books–all by the sense of feel. Likewise, although we can't see Him, we know that

God is near when we worship because we can feel His presence, or we may realize that we haven't prayed enough when someone stops us to change the order of the service because we feel that we should just keep praying. When we function at this level, we are using our spiritual senses as God intended.

Discerning Evil Spirits

If we are sensitive to what we feel, we can learn to recognize our archenemy's presence, too. We will also perceive whether he obeys or not after we command him to leave. We can even discern whether a doctrine is right or wrong when we hear it presented for the first time. John wrote:

> These things have I written unto you concerning them that seduce you. But the anointing which ye have received of him abides in you, and ye need not that any man teach you: but as the same anointing teaches you of all things, and is truth, and is no lie, and even as it hath taught you, ye shall abide in him.
> -1 John 2:26-27

Job said, "For the ear tries words, as the mouth tastes meat" (Job 34:3). Sometimes, some things just don't *sound* right.

Although the gift of "discerning of spirits" primarily operates through feeling, that's not the only way that we can "see in the dark" (see 1 Corinthians 12:10). At one time or another, God may use any one of our five spiritual senses to reveal the presence and intent of evil spirits to us.

Once, while I was praying for a lady to be delivered from cigarette addiction, a spirit suddenly rushed out of her emitting an incredibly strong tobacco smell. He advertised his presence as he left. Another time, God allowed me to see four demons leave a young man when I prayed for him to be delivered from allergies. What I saw was similar to what Eliphaz described.

> Then a spirit passed before my face; the hair of my flesh stood up: It stood still, but I could not discern the form thereof: an image was before mine eyes...
> -Job 4:15-16a

Discerning Angels

God's gifts may allow us to discern the presence of His elect angels, too. Hebrews 12:22 declares that we are surrounded by an "innumerable company" of them. Immediately after Jesus called Philip to follow Him, Philip went and found one of his friends, named Nathanael, excitedly telling him, "We have found him, of whom Moses in the law, and the prophets, did write, Jesus of Nazareth, the son of Joseph" (John 1:45).

Nathanael's response was laden with sarcasm: "Can there any good thing come out of Nazareth?" The ever practical Philip responded with, "Come and see" (John 1:46). But when Jesus saw Nathanael approaching He greeted him using a "word of knowledge," revealing Nathanael's character.

> Jesus saw Nathanael coming to him, and saith of him, Behold an Israelite indeed, in whom is no guile! Nathanael saith unto him, Whence knowest thou me? Jesus answered and said unto him, Before that Philip called thee, when thou wast under the fig tree, I saw thee. Nathanael answered and saith unto him, Rabbi, thou art the Son of God; thou art the King of Israel.
> -John 1:47-49

Nathanael was overwhelmed by the supernatural nature of Christ's greeting. He was an instant convert! Christ's testimony made a believer out of him. He knew that no one but God could have seen him praying under his fig tree earlier that morning.

His newly acquired faith in Christ's supernatural ability opened the door for even greater things! Jesus promised him that because he believed, he would soon see angels.

> Jesus answered and said unto him, Because I said unto thee, I saw thee under the fig tree, believest thou? Thou shalt see greater things than these. And he saith unto him, Verily, verily, I say unto you, Hereafter ye shall see heaven open, and the angels of God ascending and descending upon the Son of man.
> -John 1:50-51

God is impartial. He is no respecter of persons. If we believe, we can see angels, too. Our faith bridges the gap between the seen and the unseen.

> While we look not at the things which are seen, but at the things which are not seen: for the things which are seen are temporal; but the things which are not seen are eternal.
> -2 Corinthians 4:18

Past, Present, and Future

God is omniscient. "All things are naked and opened unto the eyes of him with whom we have to do" (Hebrews 4:13). Nothing is hidden from God. He knows our future equally as He knows our past. Through faith, the prophetic anointing allows us to look into the past, present, and future.

THE MASTER'S VOICE

Notice the three dimensions of Christ's ministry to Nathanael, discussed above. *Present tense:* "Behold, an Israelite indeed, in whom is no guile." *Past tense:* "Before that Philip called thee, when thou wast under the fig tree, I saw thee," and *future tense:* "Hereafter ye shall see heaven open, and the angels of God ascending and descending upon the Son of man." Thus, in three, brief snapshots, Christ gave Nathanael a present tense *view* revealing his character, a *review* of his recent past activity, and a *preview* of things yet to come.

CHAPTER FIVE
The Reproof of Instruction

> Turn you at my reproof: behold, I will pour out my spirit unto you, I will make known my words unto you.
> -Proverbs 1:23

I don't know of a single Scripture pertaining to the prophetic ministry that is more misunderstood than 1 Corinthians 14:3: "He that prophesies speaks unto men to edification, and exhortation, and comfort." Because Paul didn't specifically include rebuke or correction when he wrote this, many Christians believe that any rebuke given while prophesying is wrong. But, even a casual examination of biblical prophecy reveals that any teaching claiming the spirit of prophecy doesn't reprove and rebuke is ludicrous.

In fact, the Bible teaches that even ministering new instructions to someone amounts to a "reproof".

> For the commandment is a lamp; and the law is light; and reproofs of instruction are the way of life.
> -Proverbs 6:23

God's instructions reprove, and His reproofs give life. When God exhorts us to change and walk in righteousness, there's no way around it, it always rebukes us. But, even God's rebukes are redemptive, and His corrections edify. So it's not the content of a prophecy (i.e., whether or not it praises or rebukes) that determines whether it is proper, but rather the way it is delivered.

Love edifies. Love never criticizes; nor does it rebuke harshly. So, when we prophesy "the truth in love" (Ephesians 4:15), even God's prophetic rebukes edify.

Turn Negatives Into Positives

When God reveals something critical or negative about someone, He does so for one reason, to bring about change. He expects the one ministering to use wisdom so that whatever He is revealing will help and not hinder the one being ministered to. In other words, with few exceptions, when ministering personally, a negative truth should always be ministered in a positive way.

When ministering correction, always ask yourself, "If I were on the receiving end, how would I like this to be ministered to me?" Once, while I was ministering to a young man, God told me that he was lazy. After meditating for a moment, under the Holy Spirit's direction, I said, "The Bible says, 'The hand of the diligent maketh rich.' If you will apply yourself, God will give you success." Then, I very gently admonished him to, "be not slothful, but followers of them who through faith and patience inherit the promises" (Hebrews 6:12). As one observant brother later said, I "spoon fed" him God's correction.

Never blurt out the first thing that you hear, and it is not always wise to tell everything you know. Paul said, "I kept back nothing that was profitable unto you," (Acts 20:20) implying that he carefully weighed each revelation and gave them only that which was beneficial to them. He knew more than he revealed.

In some cases, it is best to adopt an, if-they-don't-ask,-don't-tell policy. When dealing with the immature, overzealous Christians in Corinth, Paul advised, "if any man be ignorant, let him be ignorant" (1 Corinthians 14:38). In many cases, if they are ignorant, they are unaccountable, and therefore excusable.

God is patient and merciful. He never serves any wine before it's time. He waits for a window of opportunity to open before He steps in. Until someone is ready to hear, He usually wants us to leave them alone (see Matthew 15:14). As a general rule, if your reproof or rebuke isn't going to be received, it isn't wise to give it.

The Gift of Wisdom

When God shows you something negative, simply keep looking and listening. Don't speak until He has shown you all that you need to know. God will speak plainly to you through the gift of knowledge and show or tell you *what* you are dealing with, but as you keep listening the gift of wisdom will show you *how* to deal with it. Ecclesiastes 10:10 says "wisdom is profitable to direct." As in the previous example of the lazy boy, God may give you a Scripture, parable, or even an example from your own life outlining the problem, and then another Scripture or parable revealing the solution.

Parables are valuable tools. Jesus used them constantly. Often, parables allow you to minister hard things in easy ways. When Jesus spoke to unregenerate people, He never failed to use parables. Matthew said, "without a parable spake he not unto them" (Matthew 13:34). He reserved plain speech for those He knew could and would hear.

THE MASTER'S VOICE

The Woman at the Well

Jesus' ministry to the woman at the well is a perfect example of gentle correction. Upon meeting a Samaritan woman at a public well during one of His journeys, He drew her into a discussion by asking her for a drink of water. She was amazed that He would even talk to her, since she was accustomed to the aloof, racist attitude most Jews held toward those of other races. She replied:

> How is it that thou, being a Jew, askest drink of me, which am a woman of Samaria? For the Jews have no dealings with the Samaritans.
> -John 4:9

Using her natural curiosity, Jesus drew her even deeper into His "religious" discussion, thereby opening the door to minister to her on a more personal level.

> Jesus answered and said unto her, If thou knewest the gift of God, and who it is that saith to thee, Give me to drink; thou wouldest have asked of him, and he would have given thee living water.
> -John 4:10

Her response was typical; her thoughts were still on the natural water in the well at her feet. At this point she didn't have a clue as to who He was, or what He was talking about.

> The woman saith unto him, Sir, thou hast nothing to draw with, and the well is deep: from whence then hast thou that living water?
> -John 4:11

Jesus' next comments drew the distinction between the water in the well and the living water.

Now her curiosity was too much for her. She made the specific request that He was waiting for.

> Jesus answered and said unto her, Whosoever drinketh of this water shall thirst again: But whosoever drinketh of the water that I shall give him shall never thirst; but the water that I shall give him shall be in him a well of water springing up into everlasting life. The woman saith unto him, Sir, give me this water, that I thirst not, neither come hither to draw.
> -John 4:13-15

Christ knew that she was now open to receive. Although He certainly knew that she was living in immorality, He still didn't address her situation directly. Instead He told her to, "Go, call thy husband, and come hither." Her reply revealed her heart. She said, "I have no husband" (John 14:16-17).

In essence, this woman was subtlety saying, "I'm not married. I'm available." Her whole life was consumed with trying to find Mr. Right. No doubt she was thinking, "Maybe this man is the one I've been longing for." And indeed, she was right, but not in the way that she was thinking.

Christ, alone, can fill the vast, empty void that exists in every human's heart. Natural things and natural people cannot take God's place. Spirit answers to spirit; flesh answers to flesh. The thirst of the human spirit can only be quenched by the boundless waters of God's Spirit.

> Jesus said unto her, Thou hast well said, I have no husband: For thou hast had five husbands; and he whom thou now hast is not thy husband: in that saidst thou truly. The woman saith unto him, Sir, I perceive that thou art a prophet.
> -John 4:17-19

Jesus countered her subtle attempt at flirting with Him by showing her that He discerned her true intentions. To paraphrase His reply, He said: "You're telling the truth when you say that you don't have a husband, but you're not telling the whole truth. You've had five husbands, and now you're living in adultery."

Instead of being offended at Christ's rebuke, she confirmed the accuracy of His revelation, and acknowledged the validity of His prophetic ministry. He exposed both her sin and her heart without ever alarming her and causing her to throw up her guard. By using the gift of the word of wisdom along with the gift of the word of knowledge, He successfully brought correction into her life without causing undue offense. In a few short sentences, He exposed her whole life. Her testimony was, "Come, see a man, which told me all things that ever I did" (John 4:29). One prophetic revelation changed her whole life. Christ's testimony still has the power to do the same today.

There is one more thing about His encounter with the Samaritan woman that should be noted. His ministry to her was done in private. There are certain things that should not be exposed publicly. If God reveals something to you that would embarrass or humiliate someone, simply whisper it to them, or even better, wait until you can minister to them privately. As you minister, remember to obey the golden rule; always "do unto others as you would have them do unto you."

Ministering to Leadership

Special precautions should be observed when ministering publicly to leaders, such as pastors or politicians. Obviously, a prophet shouldn't publicly reveal anything that would unnecessarily embarrass a leader before his people, but there are less obvious pitfalls to avoid as well. A prophet should carefully avoid putting a leader on the spot. For instance, if a pastor is facing an important decision, any directional word should be ministered privately or in parables, leaving room for personal interpretation. Don't make the decision for him. Allow him that privilege. Beware of ministering anything which could be construed as manipulation.

Likewise, when God reveals that He plans on relocating a pastor to a new position, it can be unsettling to the people, and quite disruptive to the minister's family. Any such revelation should be handled confidentially. Otherwise, you may unintentionally make an ill-advised, prophetic announcement to the congregation while ministering personally to the leader.

Choosing Your Words

Whether we are ministering to leaders or followers, it is impossible to keep everything confidential; however, we *can* be careful to minister with finesse. Often, just choosing the right words can make the difference between the word being received or rejected.

For example, if God shows you that someone is a fake, or that he or she is putting up a front, He may simply have you tell them that He wants them to be real. There's hope even for hypocrites if they will repent. When God shows you that someone has a tendency to be hard and legalistic, admonish them to have and give more grace, etc.

THE MASTER'S VOICE

Another example is the rather common error of using the word stubborn to mean tenacity. Although stubbornness and tenaciousness are similar, they have opposite meanings. One is negative, the other is positive. Calling someone stubborn is an insult because being stubborn is being unreasonable and self-willed. Instead, direct them to the positive potential of their nature, which is tenaciousness. If they will submit themselves to God, they can be an unmovable obstacle in Satan's path, a bulwark for righteousness and a near invincible force for hell to reckon with.

When Paul was writing to Timothy, the Holy Spirit showed him several places where Timothy was either failing in his duties or in danger of falling into sin. Among other things, Timothy was neglecting his duties to minister to the people in spiritual gifts, and like many young men, he was being tempted by money and sexual lust. Notice Paul's diplomacy and tact in dealing with him.

He approached Timothy's problems indirectly, but with firm, fatherly encouragement. For instance, rather than accusing him directly of dereliction of duty, he admonished him with, "Neglect not the gift that is in thee" (1 Timothy 4:14a). When that didn't fully do the job, he later gave him a stronger, firmer charge: "Wherefore I put thee in remembrance that thou stir up the gift of God, which is in thee by the putting on of my hands" (2 Timothy 1:6).

Then, instead of accusing Timothy of being covetous, Paul counseled him about the evils of loving money.

> But they that will be rich fall into temptation and a snare, and into many foolish and hurtful lusts, which drown men in destruction and perdition. *For*

> *the love of money is the root of all evil:* which while some coveted after, they have erred from the faith, and pierced themselves through with many sorrows. *But thou, O man of God, flee these things.*
> -1 Timothy 6:9-11a, italics mine

Likewise, concerning the danger of falling under the spell of, "silly women laden with sins, led away with divers lusts," Paul wisely advised Timothy to, "Flee also youthful lusts" (2 Timothy 3:6, 2:22a). We can all learn from Paul's tactfulness.

The Rich, Young Ruler

When Jesus encountered a self-righteous, rich, young ruler, He patiently and gently pointed out the one area of his life where he was failing God.

> And when [Jesus] was gone forth into the way, there came [a rich, young ruler] running, and kneeled to him, and asked him, Good Master, what shall I do that I may inherit eternal life? And Jesus said unto him, Why callest thou me good? there is none good but one, that is, God.
> -Mark 10:17-18

Although Jesus never directly called him self-righteous, He alluded to his basic problem by attributing all goodness to God.

> You know the commandments, Do not commit adultery, Do not kill, Do not steal, Do not bear false witness, Defraud not, Honor thy father and mother. And he answered and said unto him, Master, all these have I observed from my youth.
> -Mark 10:19-20

The young man still hadn't caught on. He continued justifying himself. While he may very well have kept those six commandments, he was breaking the most important one of all – the first one. He loved the world more than he loved God.

> *Then Jesus beholding him loved him,* and said unto him, One thing thou lackest: go thy way, sell whatsoever thou hast, and give to the poor, and thou shalt have treasure in heaven: and come, take up the cross, and follow me. *And he was sad at that saying, and went away grieved: for he had great possessions.*
> -Mark 10:21-22, italics mine

Of course Jesus loves everyone, but this was written to show us the spirit in which His correction was given. Although the rebuke was public, yet it was given in love. Jesus did exactly what His word tells us to do; He spoke "the truth in love" (Ephesians 4:15).

Exceptions to the Rule

I stated that negative things should be ministered in positive ways, with few exceptions, but there are exceptions. I once received a prophetic dream in which God warned me that I would encounter a sorcerer. (This entire dream is discussed in my second book on dreams, *Understanding the Dreams You Dream, Vol. II.*) Three years later the dream came to pass.

The first time I ministered to this man, I didn't realize that he was the sorcerer depicted in my dream. In fact, I didn't realize that he was a sorcerer at all. When I ministered to him, I saw a vision of one of his feet twisted and turned inward as though he was clubfooted. As I meditated upon what I was seeing,

God said, "He's mixed up in his doctrine." My correction was gentle and easy for him to receive.

Several months later, after I realized that he was the sorcerer God had previously warned me about, I was called upon to minister to him a second time. This time, God spoke to me and said, *"Speak plainly!"* The word He gave me to deliver was stern and direct, and I delivered it just as it was received.

Why would God make this exception? What is special about this case that's different from others?

Sorcerers are God's competitors. They compete with Him for the honor and praise of His people. God isn't very fond of them. When Philip held an evangelistic crusade at Samaria, the town's sorcerer was in the congregation along with the rest of the people.

> But there was a certain man, called Simon, which before time in the same city used sorcery, and bewitched the people of Samaria, giving out that himself was some great one: To whom they all gave heed, from the least to the greatest, saying, This man is the great power of God. And to him they had regard, because that of long time he had bewitched them with sorceries.
> -Acts 8:9-11

When Peter showed up and began laying hands on Philip's converts, Simon watched them receive the Holy Spirit and begin speaking in other tongues. His wicked heart was smitten with envy.

> And when Simon saw that through laying on of the apostles' hands the Holy Ghost was given, he offered them money, Saying, Give me also this power, that on whomsoever I lay hands, he may receive the Holy Ghost.
> -Acts 8:18-19

Tact is a keen sense of knowing what is appropriate for the situation. Sometimes, it isn't easy to tactfully deliver a negative message. Peter's method for addressing Simon was anything but tactful.

> But Peter said unto him, Thy money perish with thee, because thou hast thought that the gift of God may be purchased with money. Thou hast neither part nor lot in this matter: for thy heart is not right in the sight of God. Repent therefore of this thy wickedness, and pray God, if perhaps the thought of thine heart may be forgiven thee. For I perceive that thou art in the gall of bitterness, and in the bond of iniquity.
>
> -Acts 8:20-23

God's Competitors

God isn't kind to His competitors. He said, "I will not give my glory unto another" (Isaiah 48:11). Normally He is very patient, even with His enemies. When Herod threw Peter and James into jail, God didn't get excited. Even when Herod had James killed, He still didn't react other than to send an angel to save Peter (see Acts, chapter 12). But when Herod stole His glory by accepting the praise of His people, He didn't waste any time. God killed him!

> And upon a set day Herod, arrayed in royal apparel, sat upon his throne, and made an oration unto them. And the people gave a shout, saying, It is the voice of a god, and not of a man. And immediately the angel of the Lord smote him, because he gave not God the glory: and he was eaten of worms, and gave up the ghost.
>
> -Acts 12:21-23

That's the reason it is *correct* to say, "Thus saith the Lord" when you prophesy. God is jealous of His glory. Don't take credit for what He gives you to say. Peter warned:

> If any man speak, let him speak as the oracles of God; if any man minister, let him do it as of the ability which God giveth: that God in all things may be glorified through Jesus Christ, to whom be praise and dominion for ever and ever.
> -1 Peter 4:11

There are several more classifications of people whom God will speak to rather bluntly – but one stands out above all the rest – those who talk bluntly to others. David said:

> With the pure thou wilt shew thyself pure; and with the froward thou wilt shew thyself unsavory.
> -2 Samuel 22:27

An obstinate (froward) man cares little for the feelings of others, thus God grants him little slack.

So, when you are ministering, if the Holy Spirit directs you to speak plainly, fine, tell it like it is. But as long as you are given the choice, it's always best to temper your words. You never know which ones you may have to eat later.

> Brethren, if a man be overtaken in a fault, ye which are spiritual, restore such an one in the spirit of meekness; considering thyself, lest thou also be tempted.
> -Galatians 6:1

THE MASTER'S VOICE

Chapter Six
Submit Your Ministry

> Let your speech be always with grace, seasoned with salt, that ye may know how ye ought to answer every man.
>
> -Colossians 4:6

Thank God, that all personal prophecy isn't correction, tactful, or otherwise! In fact, correction is but a small part of the overall prophetic ministry. As we've already discussed, one of the primary purposes of the prophetic anointing is to encourage and support other ministries.

In 587 B.C., Israel went into captivity for seventy years under the rule of Nebuchadnezzar, king of Babylon, at which time both Jerusalem and Solomon's temple were destroyed. After their captivity ended, King Cyrus (Nebuchadnezzar's successor whom Isaiah prophesied of by name) issued a command to rebuild the temple. But after the foundation was laid, there arose so much opposition from Israel's enemies that all construction stopped. Then, in the days of King Darius, God raised up prophets to encourage the people to continue building.

> And the elders of the Jews built, and they prospered through the prophesying of Haggai the prophet and Zechariah the son of Iddo.
>
> -Ezra 6:14

Prosperity

God still prospers His people through the prophesying of His prophets. He said, "Believe in the

THE MASTER'S VOICE

Lord your God, so shall ye be established; believe his prophets, so shall ye prosper" (2 Chronicles 20:20). Some things never change. God, like any good father, wants the very best for His children. His heart's desire is for them to prosper.

> Beloved, I wish above all things that thou mayest prosper and be in health, even as thy soul prospers.
> —3 John 1:2

"Above all things" means that it is pretty high on His list of priorities. But notice, there's a catch. He wants us to prosper in direct proportion to our soul's prosperity. That's where the prophetic ministry comes in.

All through the Bible, when God's people fell into sin, it was the prophets' job to turn their hearts back to Him. When Israel, as a nation, turned from God their prosperity ceased. God always fulfills His promises, even when they aren't welcome. He vowed: "The wicked shall be turned into hell, and all the nations that forget God" (Psalm 9:17).

When Israel heeded the prophets' cries and repented from their evil ways, their blessings were restored. God never changes. He'll still do the same today.

When men turn their hearts toward evil, they not only forget God, they turn against anyone who reminds them of Him. Because prophets stand in God's stead against iniquity, invariably, their ministry is laden with conflict.

Ira L. Milligan

Submit Your Ministry

One of the best ways to avoid unnecessary conflict is to avoid volunteering anything personal to someone without first getting permission to speak into their life. Jesus gave us a perfect example of this when he was dining at the Pharisee's house and the woman with the alabaster box arrived. As the Pharisee watched the woman, he said to himself, "This man, if he were a prophet, would have known who and what manner of woman this is that toucheth him: for she is a sinner" (Luke 7:39). Jesus answered him saying, "Simon, I have somewhat to say unto thee;" and the Pharisee answered, "Master, say on" (Luke 7:40).

Before Jesus volunteered anything, He obtained permission to speak. Even then, He approached the situation with finesse. Instead of directly accusing Simon of being judgmental and self-righteous, He gave him a parable and asked for his opinion.

> "There was a certain creditor who had two debtors. One owed five hundred denarii, and the other fifty. And when they had nothing with which to repay, he freely forgave them both. Tell Me, therefore, which of them will love him more?" Simon answered and said, "I suppose the one whom he forgave more." And He said to him, "You have rightly judged."
> -Luke 7:41-43, NKJ

Upon obtaining the Pharisee's opinion, Jesus affirmed that his judgment was correct and then went on to offer him the logical consequences of his conclusion.

> Then He turned to the woman and said to Simon, "Do you see this woman? I entered your house; you gave Me no water for My feet, but she has washed

> My feet with her tears and wiped them with the hair of her head... You did not anoint My head with oil, but this woman has anointed My feet with fragrant oil. Therefore I say to you, her sins, which are many, are forgiven, for she loved much. But to whom little is forgiven, the same loves little." Then He said to her, "Your sins are forgiven."
>
> -Luke 7:44-48, NKJ

Under normal circumstances, contrasting a self-righteous Pharisee to a lowly harlot would undoubtedly start a fight! But, Jesus' artful rebuke left the Pharisee in stunned silence, while the harlot slipped away with radiant joy on her tear-stained face.

Thou Art the Man

Another Biblical example of using wisdom to avoid strife is seen in Nathan's ministry to King David after David's adulterous affair with Bathsheba. When David realized that Bathsheba was pregnant with his child, he tried covering up his sin by calling her husband back from war and sending him home. But his ruse didn't work. Uriah refused to go home. As a last resort, David had him killed, thinking no one would ever know. But God knew, and in this type of situation, the prophet's ministry is often brought into play. This time was no exception.

> And the Lord sent Nathan unto David. And he... said unto him, There were two men in one city; the one rich, and the other poor. The rich man had exceeding many flocks and herds: But the poor man had nothing, save one little ewe lamb, which... was unto him as a daughter. And there came a traveler unto the rich man, and he spared to take of his own flock... but took the poor man's lamb, and dressed it for the man that was come to him.

> And David's anger was greatly kindled against the man; and he said to Nathan, As the Lord lives, the man that hath done this thing shall surely die: And he shall restore the lamb fourfold, because he did this thing, and because he had no pity. And Nathan said to David, Thou art the man.
> -2 Samuel 12:1-7

Rebuking an angry king can be hazardous to your health. Nathan was taking his life into his own hands when he rebuked David. Wisdom was imperative. Tasks like this should never be taken lightly. Nathan had to get it right the first time, or else. He did, and the results were impressive.

> And David said unto Nathan, I have sinned against the Lord. And Nathan said unto David, The Lord also hath put away thy sin; thou shalt not die. Howbeit, because by this deed thou hast given great occasion to the enemies of the Lord to blaspheme, the child also that is born unto thee shall surely die.
> -2 Samuel 12:13-14

There is no substitute for wisdom. Solomon said, "Wisdom is the principal thing; therefore get wisdom: and with all thy getting get understanding" (Proverbs 4:7). When ministering prophetically, the familiar adage, "A little knowledge is a dangerous thing" is not only true, but without wisdom it can be absolutely disastrous.

Paul saw wisdom and knowledge as precious treasures, and because the two combined equals understanding, he called the full assurance that comes through understanding riches (Colossians 2:2-3). True spiritual treasures and riches await those who seek for them.

> Brethren, if a man be overtaken in a fault, ye which are spiritual, restore such an one in the spirit of meekness; considering thyself, lest thou also be tempted.
>
> -Galatians 6:1

Submission to Authority

All authority is of God. He invented it, honors it, and enforces it. No one is exempt, including prophets.

> Therefore whoever resists the authority resists the ordinance of God, and those who resist will bring judgment on themselves.
>
> -Romans 13:2; NKJ

Prophets are the same as all others. They should obey whomever they are representing. Pastors and elders are given authority in local churches. Apostles are authorized to start new churches and establish old ones, working in cooperation with existing pastors. Every minister's authority ends where his neighbor's begins. Thus, in one way or another, everyone who is in authority is under authority, and all authority is limited, except God's.

Anyone operating in the gift of prophecy should be careful to minister under proper supervision, regardless of what office they hold. Ministering secretly is out of bounds. Drawing people aside and giving them a word from the Lord often leads to harm. Submission to leaders is paramount.

If prophets are under authority, how then can they be held responsible to rebuke authorities? The answer is found in Romans 13:1a: "Let every soul be subject unto the higher powers." Some authorities are higher than others. God's word is the highest of all.

The vessel God chooses to use is immaterial. If He chooses a prophet, it's not the prophet that must be obeyed, it's God's word in the prophet's mouth that carries the authority. Donkeys are lowly creatures, yet God chose one and used it to rebuke a prophet (Numbers 22:28-30). He uses lowly prophets to rebuke high and mighty kings, or apostles, or pastors, or whomever else He decides needs correction. Whom He chooses to use is His business. Our business is to yield and obey.

What if your pastor doesn't allow spiritual gifts to operate in your church? Or, what about those churches where only select people are recognized, and the others are required to keep silent? In those cases (which hopefully are now the exception rather than the rule), seek for God's permission to join or start a small group ministry in your area. Small groups are the easiest place to learn and the best place to gain experience; however, beware of those who would rule those groups instead of lead.

Times and Places

Although your training should be under proper supervision, the best time and place to learn to prophesy is not on Sunday morning in front of hundreds of people. Large groups can be intimidating. The nonthreatening, casual atmosphere of small, home groups is a far better place to learn.

Small group ministry should be informal and relaxed. Leave formality and liturgy to the public meeting place. The atmosphere should be jubilant. Everyone should show respect for their neighbors, and give place one to another. As Paul said:

THE MASTER'S VOICE

> Let the prophets speak two or three, and let the other judge. If any thing be revealed to another that sitteth by, let the first hold his peace. For ye may all prophesy one by one, that all may learn, and all may be comforted.
> -1 Corinthians 14:29-31

No one person should dominate the conversation nor do all the ministering. The idea is everyone should have equal opportunity to share.

When properly supervised by mature leaders, small groups provide a safe haven for many people to learn how to minister in spiritual gifts and to grow in the grace of the Lord Jesus Christ. Small groups are also an excellent training camp for leadership development, and when conducted right, will be a source of numerical growth as well. They are an asset to any church.

> How is it then, brethren? When ye come together, every one of you hath a psalm, hath a doctrine, hath a tongue, hath a revelation, hath an interpretation. Let all things be done unto edifying.
> -1 Corinthians 14:26

Mistakes and Denials

Several years ago, I was invited to minister to a small men's group out in the Midwest. The men were all sitting around in a circle. Since none of them were familiar with personal prophecy, as I often do under those circumstances, after ministering to each one I stopped and asked, "Can you relate to what I've said? Does it fit?" One after another, each man nodded affirmative; several adding comments about the accuracy of their word. But when I ministered to one man, after asking him whether his word fit, he immediately denied that it did. I had mentioned that God wanted to lead him out of certain religious traditions that he had been raised in and bring him deeper into the Spirit.

His comments were, "I wasn't raised in church. I don't have any religious traditions." Puzzled, I searched the Spirit again to see if I'd misunderstood what I had seen about the man, but I saw nothing new. In fact, the Spirit showed me the exact same things all over again. I said, "Well, I must have missed it then. We all make mistakes," and went on to the next one.

As I ministered to the next man in the circle, I saw his work desk littered with printing materials. After I described what I saw and explained how God wanted him to use his natural skills to make tracts and booklets for use in ministry, he exclaimed in amazement, "You've described exactly what I do for a living. I'm a printer," and he went on to tell me just how accurate my description of the things on his desk was.

After the meeting was over, the host came over to me and said, "I don't know what got into Bob; you can't get much more religious than he is. We were raised together and went to the same church for years. He's got as much religious tradition as anyone in the room!"

It would have been a mistake for me to contest Bob's negative response. He had a right to accept or reject whatever I ministered to him. I took the humble side and although I was sure what I told him was right on target (as it was later confirmed), I conceded, anyway.

I've learned that when I minister correctly, yet the person I'm ministering to sincerely thinks I'm wrong, when I search the Spirit for them a second time, God will show me a different way to minister the same thing. That way, they can understand exactly what He means. But, if a person is obstinate and is simply rejecting the ministry through unbelief, God will not give me anything other than what He has already shown me. Usually, it's not hard for me to discern who is sincere, and who isn't. But regardless of whether someone is sincere or not, the one ministering should avoid strife whenever possible.

> And the servant of the Lord must not strive; but be gentle unto all men, apt to teach, patient
> -2 Timothy 2:24

When confronting immature and argumentative people while ministering God's gifts, Paul said, "if any man be ignorant, let him be ignorant" (1 Corinthians 14:38). The same goes for being stupid, too.

CHAPTER SEVEN
Times and Seasons

> To every thing there is a season, and a time to every purpose under the heaven: A time to be born, and a time to die; a time to plant, and a time to pluck up that which is planted; A time to kill, and a time to heal; a time to break down, and a time to build up; A time to weep, and a time to laugh; a time to mourn, and a time to dance... A time to get, and a time to lose; a time to keep, and a time to cast away; A time to rend, and a time to sew; a time to keep silence, and a time to speak; A time to love, and a time to hate; a time of war, and a time of peace... He hath made every thing beautiful in his time.
>
> -Ecclesiastes 3:1-8,11

Even as a child, I loved flying. When I was sixteen, I made up my mind that one day I would be a pilot. When I was about forty years old, after obtaining my private pilot's license, I decided to take soaring lessons. The glider I was learning to fly had a fifty-six foot wingspan and was located at a country airport with a grass runway. The landing strip was laid out between long rows of lush soybeans.

One warm, summer afternoon, while waiting for my turn to fly, I sat watching my soaring instructor training another student. They descended lower and lower as they slowly circled over the field. Misjudging his altitude, the instructor dipped one of the glider's long, graceful wings rather sharply as he banked to line up with the runway. When he did, the wingtip caught in the soybeans and the plane lurched sharply in the air. The startled pilot jerked the plane back upright, and after carefully repositioning it, he successfully executed a smooth landing. Afterward, the very embarrassed instructor climbed out and walked over mumbling, "That was one of those character building experiences!"

Building Character

We've all had a few of those, whether we wanted them or not. Some of my most memorable character building experiences involved ministering prophetically. In second Corinthians 14:29, the Bible says to judge prophecy, and with very good reason. No prophet is infallible, whether he's humble enough to admit it or not.

A few years ago, a nationally known prophet prophesied that the stock market would crash in a certain month. That month came and went while the market soared to new, record heights. A few years before, another well-known prophet prophesied that by September of the following year an earthquake would shake California and kill millions of people. They're still doing fine. One thing is certain – anyone who prophesies about earthquakes in California is sure to hit the mark somewhere, on almost any given day – but it's entirely another thing to predict the destruction of millions of people, and by a specific date, at that.

Both of those prophets made the same crucial error. Although they may have heard God accurately as to *what* was going to happen (only time will tell), they were obviously wrong as far as their *timing*.

The prophetic anointing and resultant insight is much like the telescopic lens on a newsman's camera – events appear much closer than they really are. It's easy to think that events are much nearer than they are when looking prophetically at future events. Be cautious. Prophesying events won't make them happen, regardless of who is doing the prophesying. God confirms *His* word, not ours. If you put your timeline on it, your next prediction may very well be your next lesson in humility.

God, Who is continually, "declaring the end from the beginning..., works all things after the counsel of His own will" (Isaiah 46:10a; Ephesians 1:11b), so He doesn't have a problem putting specific dates on future events, but He seldom does. Nevertheless, there are exceptions. When He banished Israel into captivity at the hands of King Nebuchadnezzar, He specified a period of seventy years. When their time was up, Daniel used Jeremiah's prophetic timetable to know when to intercede for their release. God set them free right on schedule (see Jeremiah. 25:11; Daniel 9:2-3).

A Timely Warning

The timing in Pharaoh's prophetic dream about the seven fat cows eating seven lean cows was also accurate. Joseph understood the seven fat cows to mean seven years of plenty, and the seven lean cows to represent seven years of approaching famine. He was right on both counts (see Genesis 41:1-4,26-31).

Why does God occasionally give us dates and times? Perhaps this illustration will help explain why. Once I was given a prophecy that in five years my ministry would completely change. A few weeks later, it was confirmed through a second witness who didn't know anything about the first prophecy. I wasn't expecting an *abrupt* change, so five years later (almost to the day) when God changed everything, the *way* it happened caught me completely off guard, but not the timing.

By knowing both what and when things were supposed to change, I was able to accept the way they changed despite the unpleasant circumstances that motivated the change. Nevertheless, God is The Boss, and just like He promised in Ecclesiastes 3:11, before it was over, He made everything beautiful in his time.

The Starting Line

All personal prophecy is conditional. One night, as I was ministering in our local church, I turned toward a recent high school graduate and said, "Young man, prepare yourself; God says that in two years you will be in fulltime ministry."

A few weeks later, I was sitting next to the aisle in church and this young man came strolling by me. He was full of foolishness. He was always joking and playing around. He appeared completely unconcerned about his future. Suddenly, the Holy Spirit moved on me to speak to him a second time.

I stopped him and said, "Son, you know that God's time doesn't start until you do, don't you?" He looked at me startled and said, "What do you mean?" I replied, "Don't think you can play around for two years and then expect God to suddenly jerk you up and put you into fulltime ministry. You have some preparing to do!"

When he asked what he could do to prepare, I counseled him about taking some ministry training classes that we were conducting at the time. He began attending classes. Shortly afterward, a drama team from a Bible college visited our church, and he caught their eye. At their invitation, he joined the team and began traveling with them. Later, when the founder of the Bible college met him, he gave the lad a scholarship to attend their school. When he graduated, the founder hired him to work fulltime at the Bible college. It was exactly two years from the time he started preparing.

The time element of a prophecy is the same as all other aspects of a prophecy. It, too, is conditional. When God gives you a promise, its fulfillment is totally dependent upon your willing participation.

> If ye be willing and obedient, ye shall eat the good of the land: But if ye refuse and rebel, ye shall be devoured with the sword: for the mouth of the Lord hath spoken it.
> -Isaiah 1:19-20

Soon and Very Soon

When God does choose to place a time on events, instead of stating an exact date, more often than not He will use words like: shortly, soon, very soon, etc. What does He mean when He says something will "soon" come to pass? A few days? Weeks? Years? Is His *soon* the same as ours?

When John was on the isle of Patmos, an angel showed him a vision that revealed some "things which must shortly come to pass" (Revelation 1:1). Some of the things John saw are still on hold. So far, the angel's "shortly" has lasted almost two thousand years. Why? Because with God, as far as time is concerned, everything is relative! If you need a job to support your family and God tells you not to worry, that your needs will be met "shortly," obviously, He's not talking about two thousand years. In that case, shortly can be from a few days to, at most, a few weeks.

On the other hand, if He tells a church that He is going to visit them very soon with a move of His Spirit, it may be one or more years before the revival actually comes. When prophesying to individuals about their ministry, God's "soon" may be as much as ten or twenty years away.

God is eternal. With Him, all time is relative. This means that He sees time as a sequence of events, not as revolutions of the earth around its axis. For example, Jesus ascended. The next important event is His return. Therefore, He'll be back "shortly." Of course, there are a few things which must occur in between His departure and second coming, but they are *relatively* unimportant.

Through experience, I've learned that the average prophecy will come to pass in about two years. Many, though, are not average.

CHAPTER EIGHT
Prophets of Doom and Gloom

> And Enoch also, the seventh from Adam, prophesied of these, saying, Behold, the Lord cometh with ten thousands of his saints, To execute judgment upon all, and to convince all that are ungodly among them of all their ungodly deeds which they have ungodly committed, and of all their hard speeches which ungodly sinners have spoken against him.
> -Jude 1:14-15

God has warned man of impending judgment from the very beginning of time. It will certainly come in its appointed time, but not before its time. Because of heinous sins, daily there are prophets prophesying of horrendous earthquakes, awful storms, and in short, all manners of hell, fire, and brimstone raining down upon mankind. They are correct; evil is on its way. In fact, God's judgments are so certain that Jeremiah prophesied:

> The prophet which prophesies of peace, when the word of the prophet shall come to pass, then shall the prophet be known, that the Lord hath truly sent him.
> -Jeremiah 28:9

Peace may or may not come to pass, but judgment is certain. From this it can be seen that judgment-related prophecy has its place in the overall scheme of things. It's just that it shouldn't so fill our horizons that we can see little else. Jesus set the precedent for this at the very beginning of His ministry.

THE MASTER'S VOICE

> And [Jesus] came to Nazareth... and, as his custom was, he went into the synagogue on the Sabbath day, and stood up for to read. And there was delivered unto him the book of the prophet Isaiah. And when he had opened the book, he found the place where it was written, The Spirit of the Lord is upon me, because he hath anointed me to preach the gospel to the poor; he hath sent me to heal the brokenhearted, to preach deliverance to the captives, and recovering of sight to the blind, to set at liberty them that are bruised, *To preach the acceptable year of the Lord. And he closed the book,* and he gave it again to the minister, and sat down. And the eyes of all them that were in the synagogue were fastened on him. And he began to say unto them, This day is this scripture fulfilled in your ears.
>
> —Luke 4:16-21, italics mine

The important thing about this quotation, when it comes to understanding God's attitude toward judgment, is not what Jesus read, *but what He left out.* Christ was quoting from Isaiah 61, which reads (verse 2), "To proclaim the acceptable year of the Lord, and the day of vengeance of our God; to comfort all that mourn." Jesus quit reading in the middle of the sentence.

It is wrong to emphasize the *"day of vengeance of our God"* while the Holy Spirit is still trying to emphasize the *"acceptable year of the Lord"*. God chose to complete His work of dispensing grace *before* He begins dispensing wrath! Paul said, "If you indeed have heard of the dispensation of the grace of God which was given to me to for you" (Ephesians 3:2 NKJ). The dispensation of the wrath of God is another dispensation altogether, and it's not here yet, *thank God!*

As the prophet Jonah found out, no matter how sure the promise of destruction is, God still prefers repentance. Paul said God's goodness brings about repentance, not His anger.

> Or despisest thou the riches of his goodness and forbearance and longsuffering; not knowing that *the goodness of God leads thee to repentance?*
> -Romans 2:4, italics mine

Majoring on Minors

God is not as angry as some prophets declare Him to be – at least, not yet that is. In fact, He is so merciful that even in the midst of wrath, He remembers mercy (see Habakkuk 3:2). To major on wrath and minor on mercy is the reverse of the true spirit of prophecy. James and John made that mistake. If we are wise enough to learn from their experience, we won't repeat it.

> And it came to pass, when the time was come that [Jesus] should be received up, he steadfastly set his face to go to Jerusalem, And sent messengers before his face: and they went, and entered into a village of the Samaritans, to make ready for him. And they did not receive him, because his face was as though he would go to Jerusalem. And when his disciples James and John saw this, they said, Lord, wilt thou that we command fire to come down from heaven, and consume them, even as Elias did? *But he turned, and rebuked them, and said, Ye know not what manner of spirit ye are of. For the Son of man is not come to destroy men's lives, but to save them.*
> -Luke 9:51-56, italics mine

THE MASTER'S VOICE

At the end, calamity is certain. The "more sure word of prophecy" (2 Peter 1:19), leaves no room for doubt. Noah's flood established it; Sodom and Gomorrah confirmed it; Egypt's plagues illustrated it; the prophets foresaw it; and Peter described it.

> Whereby the world that then was [in the days of Noah], being overflowed with water, perished: But the heavens and the earth, which are now, by the same word are kept in store, reserved unto fire against the day of judgment and perdition of ungodly men. But, beloved, be not ignorant of this one thing, that one day is with the Lord as a thousand years, and a thousand years as one day.
> The Lord is not slack concerning his promise, as some men count slackness; but is longsuffering to us-ward, not willing that any should perish, but that all should come to repentance. But the day of the Lord will come as a thief in the night; in the which the heavens shall pass away with a great noise, and the elements shall melt with fervent heat, the earth also and the works that are therein shall be burned up.
>
> -2 Peter 3:6-10

Isaiah foresaw something similar through the telescopic lens of his prophetic anointing: "For, behold, the darkness shall cover the earth, and gross darkness the people," but when God judged Egypt, bringing total darkness upon the nation, His own children were bathed in light. (see Exodus 10:21-23). Likewise, as Isaiah continued staring into the gloomy darkness, he saw something that made him excitedly exclaim: "but the Lord shall arise upon thee, and his glory shall be seen upon thee" (Isaiah 60:2).

Today's prophets should always remember, regardless of how dark this world gets, there's always hope for the righteous: "Jesus Christ [is, and always will be] the same yesterday, and to day, and for ever" (Hebrews 13:8). His *manner of spirit* never changes.

> For the Son of man is not come to destroy men's lives, but to save them.
>
> -Luke 9:56

THE MASTER'S VOICE

CHAPTER NINE
Prophets, True and False

> Beloved, believe not every spirit, but try the spirits whether they are of God: because many false prophets are gone out into the world.
> -1 John 4:1

N o doubt, every Christian has heard of false prophets. In fact, most Christians believe very strongly in them. It's *true* prophets whom they have trouble believing. The primary reason for this problem is, of all things, false teachers.

> But there were false prophets also among the people, even as *there shall be false teachers among you*, who privily shall bring in damnable heresies, even denying the Lord that bought them, and bring upon themselves swift destruction.
> -2 Peter 2:1, italics mine

To understand this, let's put things into perspective. The Bible refers to prophets approximately four hundred times, apostles about seventy times, teachers eighteen times, pastors eight times, and evangelists three times. Of all five ministries listed, proportionally, pastors are censored more than all the other ministries combined. They are condemned five times out of eight. Yet, they are highly respected in the Church today, and rightly so.

The fact that the Bible reproves bad pastors shouldn't make us fear to accept the ministry of good pastors, and it doesn't. But, because of an over emphasis on false prophets by paranoid teachers in the past, until recently, they've been universally rejected by the Church. It has only been in the last two decades of the twentieth century that prophets have reemerged.

Defining Prophets

Before we can identify false prophets, we need to be able to recognize the true. One leading dictionary defines a prophet as: "A person who speaks by divine inspiration or as the interpreter through whom the will of a god is expressed." That's close. If "a god" is changed to "God," it is accurate enough to use.

There are two key phrases in this modified definition: "divine inspiration" and "the will of God." The reason they are key is they separate the true from the false. A true prophet of God does not speak by his own inspiration; nor does he speak according to his own will. He expresses the Father's will, by the inspiration of the Holy Spirit. A false prophet speaks for his own gain, or according to his own will. Jesus said:

> He that speaketh of himself seeketh his own glory: but he that seeketh his glory that sent him, the same is true, and no unrighteousness is in him.
> -John 7:18

When Balaam prophesied for financial gain and fame, even though his words were true, he was declared a false prophet (see Numbers 22:16-18, 23:5-10; 2 Peter 2:15-16). It's not the content of his prophecies that determines whether a prophet is true or not, but the content of his heart. If a prophet is speaking by the inspiration of the Holy Spirit, seeking the Father's glory and His will, then Jesus said that he is "true, and no unrighteousness is in him" (John 7:18).

A prophet who misinterprets something he sees, or misunderstands something he hears and prophesies something that doesn't come to pass isn't any more false than a pastor who makes an honest mistake and teaches something that is wrong. They both simply made a mistake.

There are no perfect prophets or perfect pastors. God only uses imperfect prophets and pastors because He has no other choice. The Jewish priests collaborated with the Romans and killed the only perfect prophet and pastor that He ever had. That One is coming back, but until then, God has to use you and me.

Judging Fruit

Jesus said to judge prophets, and Paul said to judge prophecies. Prophets are judged by their fruits; prophecies are judged by their contents. Jesus said that when a prophet's heart is evil, he cannot bring forth good fruit.

> Beware of false prophets, which come to you in sheep's clothing, but inwardly they are ravening wolves. Ye shall know them by their fruits. Do men gather grapes of thorns, or figs of thistles? Even so every good tree brings forth good fruit; but a corrupt tree brings forth evil fruit. A good tree cannot bring forth evil fruit, neither can a corrupt tree bring forth good fruit.
> -Matthew 7:15-18

When men minister out of selfish motives, they are false, regardless of what office they hold or how accurate their words are. When men are sincere in their desire to please God and do His will, they are true, even when they make mistakes.

On the other hand, if a prophetic word is accurate, regardless of its source, it will still come to pass. The false prophet Balaam prophesied of the coming Messiah, and his words were true. They came to pass right on cue. On the other hand, even if a prophet is true but his words are wrong, they won't come to pass. Jeremiah asked, "Who is he that saith, and it cometh to pass, when the Lord commandeth it not?" (Lamentations 3:37). God confirms *His* word, not ours.

Three Sour Lemons

There are several varieties of sour fruits that false prophets bear, but I've noticed three in particular. Any one of the these three is enough to brand them false in my book. They are: prostituting the gifts for money; using the gifts to control and manipulate others; and displaying information obtained naturally as though it was obtained supernaturally. Occasionally, such things as immorality or spousal abuse may also be manifest, but they are usually a byproduct of the others.

1. Covetousness

When someone uses God's gifts for personal gain, he has a heart condition, commonly called covetousness. That was Balaam's problem. Elisha's servant also made that mistake. When Naaman was healed, Elisha refused to accept money for the work God had performed, but Gehazi wasn't so honest.

> But Gehazi, the servant of Elisha the man of God, said, Behold, my master hath spared Naaman this Syrian, in not receiving at his hands that which he brought: but, as the Lord lives, I will run after him, and take somewhat of him.
>
> -2 Kings 5:20

But, when he returned with his ill-gotten loot, Elisha confronted him and revealed his deception.

> But [Gehazi] went in, and stood before his master. And Elisha said unto him, Whence comest thou, Gehazi? And he said, Thy servant went no whither. And he said unto him, Went not mine heart with thee, when the man turned again from his chariot to meet thee? Is it a time to receive money, and to receive garments... and sheep, and oxen, and menservants, and maidservants? The leprosy therefore of Naaman shall cleave unto thee, and unto thy seed for ever. And he went out from his presence a leper as white as snow.
>
> -2 Kings 5:25-27

Gehazi paid a high price for the clothes and small amount of silver that he took from Naaman. Likewise, whether they are false prophets or false teachers, Peter said if they, through covetousness make merchandise of you, they are in serious trouble with God.

> And through covetousness shall [these false prophets and false teachers] with feigned words make merchandise of you: whose judgment now of a long time lingers not, and their damnation slumbers not.
>
> -2 Peter 2:3

2. Witchcraft

The second sour lemon to be aware of is ministers who use spiritual gifts to manipulate and control the lives of others. Like covetousness, this sin isn't limited to false prophets either. Control and manipulation are products of witchcraft, so regardless of what tree they grow on, they are evidence of evil roots. Never allow anyone, pastor or prophet, or any other minister, to intrude into your personal life and exercise control where he or she has no business.

Prophecy is one of the best means of knowing God's will. But, this very fact has led to many abuses and misuses of this gift. God never intended for His children to subject their personal lives to the control of others, regardless of how "gifted" they were. The gift of prophecy was not given for control, but for service.

God doesn't hand out authority indiscriminately. All legitimate authority corresponds directly to responsibility. God delegates authority for only one purpose, to enable us to fulfill our responsibilities. If a minister isn't responsible for something in a given area, he has no legitimate control in that area. For example, since a pastor is not responsible to supply food and lodging for the working members' families, he has no authority to tell them where to work – unless of course, someone is working in an X-rated club; then it becomes a moral issue.

This doesn't mean that pastors and prophets cannot address error and bring correction into the saints' personal lives. It means that submission to their ministry is strictly up to whomever is being counseled. If they see the saints in error, and they warn them in love, they have fulfilled their obligation before God. Once the saints are warned, they are individually responsible before God for their sin. God spelled out the limits of a watchman's responsibility in Ezekiel.

> Son of man, I have made thee a watchman unto the house of Israel: therefore hear the word at my mouth, and give them warning from me. When I say unto the wicked, Thou shalt surely die; and thou givest him not warning, nor speakest to warn the wicked from his wicked way, to save his life; the same wicked man shall die in his iniquity; but his blood will I require at thine hand. Yet if thou warn the wicked, and he turn not from his wickedness, nor from his wicked way, he shall die in his iniquity; but thou hast delivered thy soul.
> -Ezekiel 3:17-19

Once a word has been delivered, the messenger should forget about it. It is God's responsibility to watch over His word and fulfill it, not His messengers. To manipulate someone into fulfilling a prophecy, or to give a prophecy to influence someone into doing your own will is witchcraft, and witchcraft does not grow on trees of righteousness.

3. Hypocrisy

The third error that I've observed some prophets make is displaying information obtained naturally as though they received it by divine revelation. This is hypocrisy, and like all hypocrisy, it has only one purpose – to obtain honor from others. King Saul, who at one time "prophesied among the prophets," fell because of this flaw in his character. Even in the face of utter rejection from God, he still commanded Samuel to honor him and allow him to pretend to worship so that he could maintain the honor of his subjects.

THE MASTER'S VOICE

> And it came to pass... behold, [Saul] prophesied among the prophets... Then he said, *I have sinned: yet honor me now, I pray thee, before the elders of my people, and before Israel*, and turn again with me, that I may worship the Lord thy God.
> -1 Samuel 10:11, 15:30, italics mine

The desire for man's honor is rooted in pride. It's a basic part of human nature that must be crucified. The only honor that we should cultivate is honor from God. Jesus said, "if any man serve me, him will my Father honor" (John 12:26).

Chapter Ten
Judging Prophecy

> Let the prophets speak two or three, and let the other judge.
> -1 Corinthians 14:29

When we receive a prophecy, the Bible teaches us that before accepting it, we should first judge its authenticity. This makes it obvious that some prophecies should be rejected. Although God's word is infallible, man's word is not. How can we tell the difference between a true prophecy and one which is wrong?

When judging prophetic words, the first measuring stick to use is Scripture. A prophecy is an inspired word from God; therefore, it should be profitable in the same way that Scripture is.

> All scripture is given by inspiration of God, and is profitable for doctrine, for reproof, for correction, for instruction in righteousness.
> -2 Timothy 3:16

Regardless of how or through whom God gives His word, it will *always* conform to righteous principles. God will never instruct us to do or say something contradictory to His written word. This doesn't mean that we can always find a chapter and verse to cover any and every situation that we face, but His *righteous principles* never change. There is absolutely, "no variableness, neither shadow of turning" with God. His "manner of spirit" never wavers (see James 1:17).

There are times, though, when something may actually conform to Scripture, and still be wrong. For instance, in Luke 8:54, when James and John asked Jesus to allow them to call fire down from heaven as Elijah did, they based their request on a well-known scriptural precedent (see 2 Kings 1:9-10). But, Jesus denied their plea, because in their case, even though their request was scriptural, it still wasn't the Father's will.

Jesus said, "as I hear, I judge: and my judgment is just; because I seek not mine own will, but the will of the Father which hath sent me" (John 5:30). Christ, our mediator, filters our requests through His Father's will, but we judge His words by *our* will. Herein lies a problem. Our will and our heavenly Father's will are not always in perfect harmony, even when we think they are.

The Heart Is Deceitful

Paul said that through prophecy, God reveals the hidden secrets of the heart. Often a prophet's words are so precise they leave little room for doubt as to their accuracy. At other times, even though the word may be perfectly correct, we may feel that it isn't. One reason for this is feelings come from the heart, but we seldom know our own hearts as well as we think we do. Jeremiah 17:9 declared: "The heart is deceitful above all things, and desperately wicked: who can know it?"

It is absolutely necessary to be objective when judging a personal prophecy, and that's not always easy. For this reason, we're not always the best judge of its accuracy. Sometimes our pastor or spouse may be able to see our reflection in what the prophet has said much better than we can. That is one of the reasons Paul said to bring the *others* who are present into the judging process (see 1 Corinthians 14:29).

The Bible advises us to, "Trust in the Lord with all thine heart; and lean not unto thine own understanding" (Proverbs 3:5). If we trust our feelings we may judge a prophecy as wrong, even when in reality it is directly from God. Feelings may be real, but they aren't always right. If our hearts desire is to please our heavenly Father, we won't have any trouble judging whether a personal prophecy is from Him or not. If our heart is wrong, we may reject a word that is directly from the Father's heart without realizing it. This is true whether we are judging the accuracy of a prophetic word, the wisdom of someone's counsel, or the correctness of a doctrinal teaching.

God Is in the Details

You've probably heard the expression, "The devil's in the details." Well, he's not the only one; God is too, especially where judging prophecy is concerned. Because we are prone to, "hear what we want to hear," we may actually think a prophecy failed when in reality, it didn't. Moses' rather amusing reaction to a failed prophetic word is a prime example of this quirk of human nature.

God sent Moses to Egypt with instructions to promise the Israelites deliverance from slavery and a land of their own. He also told him that while he was there to go by and tell Pharaoh to set the slaves free, and then, almost as an afterthought, He said: "And I am sure that the king of Egypt will not let you go, no, not by a mighty hand" (Exodus 3:19).

Moses obeyed, delivered the messages as instructed, and then got rebuffed by both parties! Frustrated, he reported back to God.

> For since I came to Pharaoh to speak in thy name, he hath done evil to this people; *neither hast thou delivered thy people at all.*
> -Exodus 5:23, italics mine

Why was Moses surprised? Pharaoh did exactly what God said he would do.

Moses' complaint reveals that he only heard part of the prophecy. He completely overlooked one important detail – "The king... will not let you go." Moses' report should have stated, "Everything is going exactly as planned. What's the next step?" But it didn't, because Moses heard only what he wanted to hear. We all share this too common, human trait.

Two or Three Witnesses

Another important rule for judging prophecy (and one way to counter some of the aforementioned problems) is this – God's word will always be confirmed through more than one witness. All rhema words from God should have at least two witnesses. Paul said: "In the mouth of two or three witnesses shall every *word* be established" (2 Corinthians 13:1, italics mine). In this Scripture, the word translated *word* in the Greek is *rhema*, meaning utterance. Every divinely inspired utterance will be established through at least two witnesses.

There are several reasons for God putting this rule into place. One reason is safety. Solomon said, "In the multitude of counselors there is safety" (Proverbs 11:14). We may stubbornly disagree with one witness, but if we hear two or three repeating the same thing, it becomes obvious that we may be wrong in rejecting what we've been told.

Another reason for more than one witness is that God seldom gives us His whole counsel through only one messenger. Paul said, "We prophesy in part" (1 Corinthians 13:9). This means the second part (and possibly even the third and fourth) will be given to us in other ways, or through different people. It's not until we have all the parts assembled that we have the whole counsel of God. And, possibly another reason for more than one witness is having to wait for the second witness to show up teaches us patience.

The Final Test

When a prophecy conforms to Scripture, is confirmed by other witnesses and in every other way appears true. Before receiving the final seal of approval, it must pass one last test. If *we* meet God's conditions, a prophecy which is truly *His* word will *always* come to pass. Moses said:

> And if thou say in thine heart, How shall we know the word which the Lord hath not spoken? When a prophet speaketh in the name of the Lord, *if the thing follow not, nor come to pass, that is the thing which the Lord hath not spoken, but the prophet hath spoken it presumptuously*: thou shalt not be afraid of him.
> -Deuteronomy 18:21-22, italics mine

The Hebrew word translated presumptuously here literally means pride or arrogance. When a prophet speaks from the pride of life, instead of from the spirit of prophecy, he misses God and brings confusion to those he ministers to. God will not fulfill a prophet's word spoken presumptuously. "Who is he that saith, and it cometh to pass, when the Lord commandeth it not?" (Lamentations 3:37).

Although some prophets may appear infallible, and some may foolishly think they are, Paul said, "let God be true, and every man a liar" (Romans 3:4). Those whom God has honored by entrusting them with His wonderful gift must be ever watchful to purify their hearts from pride. The desire for the honor of man always brings a snare. Failing to crucify the desire for man's praise and favor will rob us of God's eternal reward.

A personal word from God can direct us in times of indecision, comfort us in times of sorrow, and encourage us when we are facing seemingly insurmountable problems. There is no other ministry that can do what the prophetic does.

Although Satan wars against God's prophets and tries to make their prophetic promises fail, he cannot defeat God. God said that He watches over His word to fulfill it (see Jeremiah 1:12). God is faithful. His word is His bond. When we stand upon His word, we are standing upon the one thing that is eternal. Although we can and do fail, God's word never fails.

CHAPTER ELEVEN
Elijah and Elisha

> Behold, I will send you Elijah the prophet before the coming of the great and dreadful day of the Lord: And he shall turn the heart of the fathers to the children, and the heart of the children to their fathers, lest I come and smite the earth with a curse.
>
> -Malachi 4:5-6

Elijah is coming! In fact, he has already come, left for a while, and is back again to stay for a season. Please let me explain. Before Jesus was born, an angel appeared to a priest named Zacharias to announce John the Baptist's birth. He prophesied that John would minister in the spirit and power of Elijah.

> And [John] shall go before him in the spirit and power of Elijah, *to turn the hearts of the fathers to the children, and the disobedient to the wisdom of the just;* to make ready a people prepared for the Lord.
>
> -Luke 1:17, italics mine

After Christ began His ministry, the disciples questioned Him about Malachi's end-time prophecy, which foretold of Elijah's return. Jesus explained that this prophecy was partially fulfilled in John the Baptist's ministry, but He also promised a future fulfillment.

> And his disciples asked him, saying, Why then say the scribes that Elijah must first come? And Jesus answered and said unto them, *Elijah truly shall*

> *first come, and restore all things.* But I say unto you, That Elijah is come already, and they knew him not, but have done unto him whatsoever they listed. Likewise shall also the Son of man suffer of them.
>
> -Matthew 17:10-12, italics mine

When Jesus said, "Elijah truly shall first come", He was telling us, "You haven't seen the last of him yet." So, John the Baptist, who ministered in the spirit and power (anointing) of Elijah at the time of Jesus' first appearance was one fulfillment of Malachi's prophecy, and today's prophets who are forerunners of Christ's second coming are fulfilling Malachi's prophecy a second time. So, Elijah is back on the job, and much needed.

The Elijah Anointing

Malachi said that the purpose of Elijah's anointing was to, "turn the heart of the fathers to the children, and the heart of the children to their fathers," and the angel announced that John would, "turn the hearts of the fathers to the children, and the disobedient to the wisdom of the just." In each case, they were sent to minister to those who were prodigals, backsliders, those who had gotten off track. They were sent to convict and convert the disobedient sinners among God's people – "lest [God] come and smite the earth with a curse," and we *definitely* want to avoid that!

The Elisha Anointing

What about Elisha? Where does he fit into this picture? Elisha was Elijah's replacement. After God successfully brought Israel to repentance through Elijah's ministry, He sent him to anoint Elisha "to be prophet in thy room" (1 Kings 19:16). In the same way that Elijah was sent to minister conviction to bring repentance, it was Elisha's job to minister faith to bring blessings.

There's one major difference between these two men's anointings – a difference that foreshadowed the transition from Law to grace. Elijah called fire down from heaven and destroyed his enemies, and Elisha blessed his enemies by feeding them and setting them free (see 2 Kings 1:9-10, 6:15-22; Matthew 5:43-43). Of the two possibilities, the Scriptures teach that God prefers blessings over fire any day. In fact, He would rather bless twice as much (at least, that is what Elisha's ministry appears to indicate).

A Double Portion

Right before Elijah was caught up into heaven, he asked Elisha what he could do for him before he left.

> And it came to pass, when they were gone over [the Jordan river], that Elijah said unto Elisha, Ask what I shall do for thee, before I be taken away from thee. And Elisha said, I pray thee, let a double portion of thy spirit be upon me. And he said, Thou hast asked a hard thing: nevertheless, *if thou see me when I am taken from thee, it shall be so unto thee; but if not, it shall not be so.* And it came to pass, as they still went on, and talked, that, behold, there appeared a chariot of fire, and horses of fire, and parted them both asunder; and Elijah went up by a whirlwind into heaven. *And Elisha saw it...*
>
> -2 Kings 2:9-12a, italics mine

The only condition Elisha had to meet was to see Elijah taken up (which Elisha did). After Elijah was gone, Elisha smote the waters of the Jordan as he had seen Elijah do a short time before. "Where is the Lord God of Elijah?" he cried, and the mighty river rolled back. Elisha had his heart's desire, a double portion of Elijah's anointing.

> He took up also the mantle of Elijah that fell from him, and went back, and stood by the bank of Jordan; And he took the mantle of Elijah that fell from him, and smote the waters, and said, Where is the Lord God of Elijah? and when he also had smitten the waters, they parted hither and thither: and Elisha went over.
> -2 Kings 2:13-14

When Elijah ascended, his mantle fell back to earth. His mantle represents his anointing.

> But unto every one of us is given grace according to the measure of the gift of Christ. Wherefore he saith, *When he ascended up on high, he led captivity captive, and gave gifts unto men.*
> -Ephesians 4:7-8, italics mine

On the day of Pentecost, Christ dropped His mantle upon the waiting disciples. When it fell on them, they spoke in tongues, and Peter began prophesying.

> For these are not drunken, as ye suppose...But this is that which was spoken by the prophet Joel; And it shall come to pass in the last days, saith God, I will pour out of my Spirit upon all flesh: and your sons and your daughters shall prophesy, and your young men shall see visions, and your old men shall dream dreams: And on my servants and

on my handmaidens I will pour out in those days of my Spirit; and they shall prophesy.

-Acts 2:15-18

When Peter rebuked Simon the sorcerer, he was ministering in the spirit and power of Elijah. When he raised Dorcas from the dead, he was ministering one of the blessings of Elisha's double portion. Jesus promised:

> Verily, verily, I say unto you, He that believeth on me, the works that I do shall he do also; and greater works than these shall he do; because I go unto my Father.
>
> -John 14:12

THE MASTER'S VOICE

Chapter Twelve
Prophetic Dreams and Visions

> And he said, Hear now my words: If there be a prophet among you, I the Lord will make myself known unto him in a vision, and will speak unto him in a dream.
>
> -Numbers 12:6

Several years ago I was working as an appliance repairman for a large department store in central Louisiana. My route stretched over fifty miles out into the country, covering numerous small towns and communities. I knew the route well, including the location of various churches along the way.

One Wednesday morning I dreamed that I was preaching in one of those country churches. Although I had never been inside the church, I later discovered that in the dream I saw it as it actually existed. I was preaching from the text, "God that made the world and all things therein, seeing that he is Lord of heaven and earth, dwells not in temples made with hands" (Acts 17:24).

I was exhorting the people that even though our church buildings may be necessary, they were but tools to be used in building the true temple of God. Our primary attention should be on the people, not buildings. As Paul said in his letter to the Ephesians, *we* are the temple. In Christ, we "are built together for a dwelling place of God in the Spirit" (Ephesians 2:21-22 NKJ).

When I awoke, even though the church was about forty miles away, I decided to pay it a visit. That evening, when I walked into the sanctuary, I realized that it looked exactly as it appeared in my dream. Before I could even find a seat someone recognized me and said, "Look, here's a preacher. He can preach tonight." They told me their pastor had called in sick and they were questioning what to do. Accepting their invitation, I delivered the message that God had given me in my dream.

I was completely unaware that the church had recently started a building project, which had become a source of strife and division among its members. My message was directly from God, exhorting them to set their priorities straight.

As I travel, it is not uncommon for God to give me messages through dreams for various churches in which I minister . God knows what they need to hear. All I have to do is be His messenger boy.

Divinely inspired dreams and visions are found in almost every book in the Bible. There are fifty-eight references to dreams, and eighty-three references to visions in Scripture. Yet, until a few years ago, both were almost non-existent in most Christian circles.

God is changing all that. In these last days, He is pouring out His Spirit just as He promised. Young men are seeing visions, and old men are dreaming dreams.

> And it shall come to pass afterward, that I will pour out my spirit upon all flesh; and your sons and your daughters shall prophesy, your old men shall dream dreams, your young men shall see visions.
>
> -Joel 2:28

In this Scripture, young men depicts those who are born again, and old men simply refers to the unregenerate, natural man. Both genders and all ages are accepted by Him. These newly restored dreams and visions are imparting a wealth of spiritual knowledge to His Church.

Besides showing us what we can expect ahead, prophetic dreams confirm certain changes that occur as we travel along life's highway. Through our dreams, God often reveals secular job/career changes, geographical moves, and even such things as changes in church and ministry relationships. It's comforting to be able to see around the next corner before we get there!

God can impart the word of knowledge and the word of wisdom to us easier while we are asleep than when we are awake. When we are awake, our conscious mind always questions and doubts whatever our spirit is receiving. When we are asleep, our minds are unconscious, so God can say whatever He wants to say without interference.

But, God has a problem. Our society has taught us that dreams don't mean anything, so the Church isn't listening. Since most dreams are symbolic and have to be interpreted before anyone knows what they actually mean, many Christians don't recognize that God is the one talking. Many Christians are treating their dreams as junk mail. They simply toss them into the trashcan of forgetfulness.

Recording Dreams

Most personal prophecies are recorded for future review and use, but most prophetic dreams are forgotten almost as soon as they are received. The only practical way to remedy this problem is to start a dream journal. After a dream is recorded, you can pray and meditate for God to give you the interpretation.

THE MASTER'S VOICE

Once you understand the message the dream contains, you should treat it the same as any other prophecy. Of course, when a dream foretells the future, it is usually hard to interpret – but even so – if you record it so that you can review it regularly, in the time of its fulfillment it can be quite helpful.

The biggest problem in interpreting divinely inspired dreams is being able to put them into their proper settings. To obtain the setting, ask yourself, "What *subject* is this dream talking about? *Whom* is it addressing? What kind of *message* does it contain? Is it a warning? Does it answer a question that I've asked, or give me instructions to do the Father's will? Or is it possibly a confirmation of something that He has previously shown me?"

Knowing a dream's subject and whom it addresses enables you to apply it correctly. Once you determine what it's talking about, and whom it refers to, then you should search to see if there is something in the dream that depicts time.

For example, in Pharaoh's prophetic dream about the seven fat cows eating seven lean cows that we discussed in Chapter Seven, the cows and their condition referred directly to Egypt's economy. They represented seven years of prosperity and seven years of famine, respectively. Their number showed the duration of each period of time.

How did Joseph know the cows represented years? They came up out of the river, and flowing streams and rivers often portray the passage of time. Without Joseph's interpretation and pharaoh's wise reaction, Egypt would have been destroyed, God's will for Jacob and his descendants would have been thwarted, and history would have recorded a completely different story. Such is the power of dreams.

Recommended Books on Dreams

I've written two books on dreams: *Understanding the Dreams You Dream* and *Understanding the Dreams You Dream, Vol. II*. For each book, I used both personal and biblical dreams to teach the proper method of interpreting dreams, including the dream about the sorcerer referred to in Chapter Five. Because of the complexity of this subject, I recommend both of these books for an in-depth study of prophetic dreams.

THE MASTER'S VOICE

CHAPTER THIRTEEN
His Potential in You

> When Jesus then lifted up his eyes, and saw a great company come unto him, he saith unto Philip, Whence shall we buy bread, that these may eat? And this he said to prove him: *for he himself knew what he would do.*
>
> -John 6:5-6, italics mine

In 1972, when God first called me a prophet, I was dumbfounded. I knew there was absolutely no way that I could ever live up to the high and lofty ideal that I held concerning prophets. He already knew my abilities before He called me, and had planned on doing it Himself from the beginning. In the process of working out His will in my life, He has amazed me, startled me, even scared me, but seldom disappointed me.

God is like a doting father who allows his young son to try something that he knows he cannot do. After the boy surrenders, He reaches over and does it for him. God delights in demonstrating His amazing ability to do the impossible.

In his first letter to the Corinthians, Paul said that God chooses weak things to confound things, which are strong.

> But God hath chosen the foolish things of the world to confound the wise; and God hath chosen the weak things of the world to confound the things which are mighty; And base things of the world, and things which are despised, hath God chosen, yea, and things which are not, to bring to nought things that are: That no flesh should glory in his presence.
>
> −1 Corinthians 1:27-29

Feeding the Five Thousand

A perfect example of this is when Jesus was faced with five thousand hungry followers, and the bakery was closed. (Or, according to Philip, it may as well have been.)

> When Jesus then lifted up his eyes, and saw a great company come unto him, he saith unto Philip, Whence shall we buy bread, that these may eat? *And this he said to prove him: for he himself knew what he would do.* Philip answered him, Two hundred pennyworth of bread is not sufficient for them, that every one of them may take a little. One of his disciples, Andrew, Simon Peter's brother, saith unto him, There is a lad here, which hath five barley loaves, and two small fishes: but what are they among so many?
>
> −John 6:5-9, italics mine

"Five loaves and two small fishes, but what are they among so many?" Not much! That is, not much until they are placed into the hands of the Master. Although Jesus pretended to question Philip about the bakery, His plans were already made. He would take something weak and make it strong. He would take something inferior and make it superior. He would use that which was lacking to meet every need. He would take something so insignificant that it was nothing, and make it so plentiful that in the end, there would be an abundance. And He would do it all without ever breaking a sweat. All Jesus needed was their cooperation.

> And Jesus said, Make the men sit down. Now there was much grass in the place. So the men sat down, in number about five thousand. And Jesus took the loaves; and when he had given thanks, he distributed to the disciples, *and the disciples to them that were set down;* and likewise of the fishes *as much as they would.*
> -John 6:10-11, italics mine

Can't you see the utter amazement on their faces? No, not on the crowds' faces – the disciples'! They were the one's serving the food. It was their hands in which the bread multiplied.

John watched in awe. He said they ate as much as they would. There was one man that day who saw a greater miracle than any of the others. He was the hungriest man in the crowd. He was the one who kept coming back for more. God never let him down.

> When they were filled, he said unto his disciples, Gather up the fragments that remain, that nothing be lost.
> -John 6:12

God is not stingy, and not wasteful. The remnant tells of His goodness; the fragments testify of His generosity. He's still looking for people of faith who will cooperate with Him. Although it's true that you can do nothing of yourself, if you can break a loaf of bread, you can work a miracle. If you can serve a table, you can reveal His goodness to the world.

When God calls you into His service, He addresses His potential in you, never your potential in Him. It's not who *you* are in Christ that counts; it's Who *He* is in you that makes the difference.

Gideon's Call

When God called Gideon into His service, he was probably the last one that we would have chosen. The angel's words were incredible even to Gideon: "And the angel of the LORD appeared unto him, and said unto him, The LORD is with thee, thou mighty man of valor" (Judges 6:12). You can almost hear Gideon's startled reply, "Who, me?"

He responded exactly as you or I would under those same circumstances. "Oh my Lord, wherewith shall I save Israel? Behold, my family is poor in Manasseh, and I am the least in my father's house" (Judges 6:15).

In essence, Gideon said, "I don't have any money, and I'm not well-known. You've called the wrong guy." But God's plans were already laid. He was only waiting for Gideon's confession of his own inadequacy. The angel's response reveals His plan.

> And the LORD said unto him, *Surely I will be with thee*, and thou shalt smite the Midianites as one man.
> -Judges 6:16, italics mine

All God needed was Gideon's cooperation. Gideon's real job was simple. He was there to tell the people Who really delivered them – not to do the job itself. Nevertheless, God allowed him to share the credit, even from the beginning. By all appearances, Gideon would be a one-man army:

The plan worked. As soon as Gideon faced what he feared and obeyed God, God sent confusion into his enemies' camp and, "set every man's sword against his fellow, even throughout all the host: and the host fled" (Judges 7:22).

God did it again! He took something weak and made it strong. He took something inferior and made it superior. He used that which was lacking and met every need. He took something so insignificant that it was nothing, and yet made it so plentiful that in the end there was an abundance. God did it all without ever breaking a sweat. All He needed was Gideon's cooperation.

A Willing Vessel

When Jesus called Peter and Andrew to leave their nets and follow Him, He promised to make them "fishers of men" (Matthew 4:18-19). We are not sure about Andrew, but we have every reason to believe that Peter was anything other than holy and righteous at the time he was called. He certainly was not a stranger to swearing (see Matthew 26:73-74).

In other words, when Jesus spoke to Peter, He was prophesying to a sinner – yet, He didn't say a word about repenting. Instead, He prophesied to him about his ministry. He was talking to Peter about evangelizing and Peter wasn't even saved yet!

When God calls us into His service, His intention is to make us into whatever He wants us to be. He's not expecting us to already look like the finished product. All He's looking for is a willing vessel. He needs only one thing, our cooperation.

In the same manner that Peter left his nets and followed Christ, I've seen sinners surrender their

THE MASTER'S VOICE

hearts to God even as they were being prophesied to. I've also seen rebellious saints change overnight because God assured them they were loved and needed.

When Jesus sent the disciples ahead to get the colt for Him to ride, He told them where to find the animal and to "loose him and bring him, And if any man say unto you, Why do ye this? say ye that the Lord hath need of him; and straightway he will send him hither" (Mark 11:2b-3). The colt was unbroken, but willingly submitted to the Master's touch.

When God says, "I have need of you", there is something supernatural that takes place in a man's heart. There are many more out there like Peter who are unbroken, untrained sinners, just waiting for the Master's touch. Through the prophetic ministry, He has given us the power to loosen them and bring them to Him.

CHAPTER FOURTEEN
Walking on His Word

> Where the word of a king is, there is power.
> -Ecclesiastes 8:4

No doubt, the other disciples watched in stunned disbelief as Peter frantically climbed over the side of the boat. One can almost see the boat as it twists and groans beneath them, its bow rising and falling violently with each passing swell. The sea churning and surging as its waves crash savagely against their craft, soaking the eleven to the bone as they cling to their oars and pull with every ounce of strength they have, *and Peter got out of the boat!*

Peter probably clung to the side for a brief moment before gingerly stepping out onto the dark waters. Incredibly, he walked. The eleven saw him rise and descend on the waves as he faded into the night, *walking on the sea*. All because the Master had beckoned and said, "Come" (see Matthew 14:24:28). Just one word – that was all Peter needed. Defying gravity and sustaining Peter was nothing for God. He "upholds all things by the word of His Power" (Hebrews 1:3).

When Gabriel first visited Mary, she was shocked at his announcement – her, have a child? She was a virgin! Gabriel explained that nothing is impossible with God (see Luke 1:37). If He declares it, He can and will do it!

If God tells you to do something, get with it. His word is all you need. He's able to sustain you, regardless of what your needs may be. His supply is boundless. His riches are unsearchable. Paul said that he was called to preach the unsearchable riches of Christ.

> Unto me, who am less than the least of all saints, is this grace given, that I should preach among the Gentiles the unsearchable riches of Christ.
> -Ephesians 3:8

We can't hang onto the boat and still see God's word fulfilled in our lives. Our full participation and cooperation are required. Paul said that although all of God's promises are solid and sure, we still have a part to play in their fulfillment.

> For the Son of God, Jesus Christ, who was preached among you by us, even by me and Silvanus and Timotheus, was not yea and nay, but in him was yea. For all the promises of God in him are yea, and in him Amen, unto the glory of God *by us*.
> -2 Corinthians 1:19-20, italics mine

Many Christians are unaware that most personal prophecies aren't telling them what God is *going* to do. Instead, the prophecies are telling them what He *wants* to do. Paul said, where there are prophecies, they shall fail (1 Corinthians 13:8). Without faith and full cooperation from those who receive them, many prophecies will not come to pass even if they are issued straight from the throne of God.

The Revelation of His Will

A prophecy is the revelation of the will of God under existing, stated or implied conditions. God reveals His will through His word. This is true whether we receive His word by reading the Bible, hearing inspired sermons, receiving personal prophecy, or dreaming prophetic dreams.

Once we have evaluated a prophecy and judged it as authentic, the first thing we should do is pray. If we agree with it, we should pray for God to bring it to pass. If we disagree, and would like for His will to change, we must pray accordingly. If the prophecy is a warning of impending judgment, we should repent and seek to change the conditions that are displeasing Him.

Conditions For Fulfillment

All personal prophecy is conditional. When Jonah cried out against Nineveh, the city was ripe for destruction. But, when the king heard the prophetic word, he believed God. He called a public fast and began to pray. As a result, the conditions changed, and to Jonah's dismay, the promised destruction never materialized. Instead, God spared the city (Jonah 3:5-10).

On the other hand, when Mary received her personal prophecy concerning the birth of Jesus, she said: "Behold the handmaid of the Lord; be it unto me according to thy word" (Luke 1:38). As a result, in due process of time, Christ was born.

Some prophecies fail because those who receive them fail to meet God's conditions. When Paul reminded Timothy about the prophecies that he had received during his ordination, he exhorted him to, "Meditate upon these things; give thyself wholly to them; that thy profiting may appear to all" (1 Timothy 4:15). God desires heartfelt participation: "give thyself wholly" to what He is doing in your life. He doesn't like halfhearted commitment.

THE MASTER'S VOICE

One of the best examples of this is the children of Israel. God promised them Canaan land, but they refused to believe Him when faced with the difficulties of the conquest. God's condition for the fulfillment of His promise was for them to overcome their fears and act upon His word. They refused. The penalty for stubborn refusal to believe and obey is always the same – God withdraws His promise (see Hebrews 3:18-19, 4:1). A prophetic promise will always challenge our faith and test our obedience.

Although Moses' prophecy failed in its fulfillment, God's word never fails in its purpose. Isaiah said:

> So shall my word be that goes forth out of my mouth: it shall not return unto me void, but it shall accomplish that which I please, and it shall prosper in the thing whereto I sent it.
> -Isaiah 55:11

God's word tries us, proves us, changes us, sustains us, and finally, judges us (see Psalms 105:19; John 15:3; 12:48). Those who meet His conditions and obey His word receive His promises. Those who stumble in battle, lose.

> If ye be willing and obedient, ye shall eat the good of the land: But if ye refuse and rebel, ye shall be devoured with the sword.
> -Isaiah 1:19-20

True faith always produces victory. "For... this is the victory that overcomes the world, even our faith" (1 John 5:4).

Chapter Fifteen
The Trial of Your Faith

> Beloved, think it not strange concerning the fiery trial which is to try you, as though some strange thing happened unto you.
> -1 Peter 4:12

We were visiting a church in Oklahoma again, but this time things were different. It had been four years since God had startled me by calling me a prophet. Those four years had been exciting, and rough! During that time I learned one thing that stood out above everything else – everyone who calls himself a Christian doesn't necessarily want to hear what God has to say. As long as God stays in the Bible, everything's all right. But let Him get out and start walking around making His presence known, then watch out!

There were two other ministers visiting with me that night, in fact, the same two who were with me on my last trip to Oklahoma. We were hungry to see a move of God, so we had agreed together to fast four days for the service. We weren't disappointed; God showed up. His Spirit came upon me so strong that I fell to the floor, something commonly called being "slain in the Spirit." I had experienced it a few times before when the Holy Spirit's presence came into our midst extra powerfully. I lay quietly, enjoying the warm sensation of the Holy Spirit's presence. Suddenly, the Master spoke, "Arise and prophesy."

Previous to this I had spent several years studying and learning to minister in the gifts of the Spirit. Discerning of spirits, tongues, interpretation, prophecy, healing, my wife and I had sought them all. God hadn't disappointed us, either. During that time we grew by leaps and bounds, but at the same time we faced unbelievable hostility and opposition. On two occasions, in two different churches, when a message in tongues came forth, the pastors actually had the people stand up and sing to drown out my wife as she began interpreting the messages. And that was only the tip of the iceberg.

After two especially difficult years of that kind of rejection, I'd had enough – I quit! I decided that prophecy wasn't necessary. Teaching and preaching the Bible was enough. And it was enough for me, but not for God.

Robbed by Satan

The Master spoke the second time: "Arise and prophesy." It was a no-nonsense, *get up and do what I said* command. Suddenly I realized what Satan had done. I'd been robbed! I had yielded to him and laid down the one gift that I valued the most, the gift of prophecy. The more I thought about it, the angrier I became.

I stood up, and the Holy Spirit began to flood my spirit with words. I started prophesying, and like the elders of Moses, I did not cease. Satan may have won the first round, but I vowed that he wasn't going to win the second one. I learned a valuable lesson that night. You have to seek God for His gifts to receive them, and you have to fight the devil if you want to keep them.

Peter won a tremendous victory over doubt and fear the night he defied logic and climbed out of his boat onto that stormy sea; however, his victory was short-lived. Notice how the story ends.

> And when Peter was come down out of the ship, he walked on the water, to go to Jesus. *But when he saw the wind boisterous, he was afraid; and beginning to sink, he cried, saying, Lord, save me.* And immediately Jesus stretched forth his hand, and caught him, and said unto him, O thou of little faith, wherefore didst thou doubt? And when they were come into the ship, the wind ceased.
>
> -Matthew 14:29-32, italics mine

When Peter saw the wind's fury, he came to his senses – his natural senses, that is. As long as he went by what Christ said, he walked. When he quit walking by faith and began to pay attention to what his natural senses were saying, he sank. Fear robbed him. Fear is Satan's first line of attack.

When God sent Joshua into Canaan, He told him there were seven nations for him to destroy. But, three days before going in, God condensed the seven down into one nation – the Hittites. (The word *Hittite* means terror [Joshua 1:4].) God knew that if the Israelites could overcome their fears, the other nations would be bread and butter for them.

If Satan can steal your faith, he has your gift. Besides trying to paralyze you with fear, he will harass you, accuse you falsely, oppose you, tell you that everything you are doing is wrong – the list is endless. He hates God, every manifestation of God, and every representative of God. You will not get away with ministering in the supernatural without a fight. Prepare for it, but don't allow yourself to develop PMS (paranoid mental state) in the process, or you won't be fit to fulfill your calling.

THE MASTER'S VOICE

Tactics of Satan

Paul said we are not ignorant of Satan's devices, and he uses several (see 2 Corinthians 2:11). His favorite is *entry level warfare*, which often includes, but is not limited to, *intimidating, bargaining,* and *challenging*. He tried using all four of these on the Master. They weren't effective on Christ, but they might be on you and me if we aren't aware of how they work.

The first, entry level warfare, is found throughout the Scriptures. Satan tried killing Moses while he was still a baby, and even though it failed the first time, he tried it again when Jesus was born. It's a lot easier to defeat defenseless babies than grown men.

The same tactic is also seen in the book of Joshua. Satan knew it would be easier to stop Joshua at the beginning of his advance into Canaan than it would be to wait until he was well entrenched in the land. So, shortly after Joshua defeated Jericho, Satan rallied his troops against him (see Joshua 9:1-2). Of course, this didn't work either. However, Satan doesn't give up easily.

Using the same logic, Satan tried to stop Jesus at the beginning of His advance, too. The devil knew Jesus was going to be trouble, so he threw everything in his arsenal at Him. First, he tried intimidation. Satan *ordered* Christ to turn stones into bread.

> And the devil said unto him, If thou be the Son of God, command this stone that it be made bread.
> -Luke 4:3

So, what's wrong with that? Christ had the power, and He was hungry, wasn't He? The answer is simple, "to whom ye yield yourselves servants to obey, his servants ye are to whom ye obey" (Romans 6:16).

It's the same old trick the devil used on Eve. If you do what he says, you become his servant. Jesus didn't fall for it.

Then Satan reached deeper into his bag of tricks and came up with a bargain. Or, he tried to sell it as one, anyway.

> And the devil, taking him up into an high mountain, showed unto him all the kingdoms of the world in a moment of time. And the devil said unto him, All this power will I give thee, and the glory of them: for that is delivered unto me; and to whomsoever I will I give it. If thou therefore wilt worship me, all shall be thine.
> -Luke 4:5-7

Jesus wasn't buying the scheme. You can't afford to either. Satan's price is too high, and if you buy into his lie, it will cost you everything God has reserved for you. But, there's one thing you can count on – whether you're willing to buy or not is immaterial – Satan is going to offer it to you, anyway.

Satan's next tactic, though certainly not his last, was to challenge Christ, or as we used to say when we were kids, he double-dog dared Him.

> And he brought him to Jerusalem, and set him on a pinnacle of the temple, and said unto him, If thou be the Son of God, cast thyself down from hence: For it is written, He shall give his angels charge over thee, to keep thee: And in their hands they shall bear thee up, lest at any time thou dash thy foot against a stone.
> -Luke 4:9-11

One thing should be obvious by now; it's not what Satan tells you to do that matters, it's the fact that he's the one giving the orders. Every attempt he made to get Jesus to yield failed because Christ saw right through his ruse. As the Master said, "Thou shalt worship the Lord thy God, and him only shalt thou serve [obey]" (Luke 4:8).

Notice Satan's threefold strategy; his first attempt was based on Christ's physical needs. Jesus was hungry. His second thrust appealed to the carnal desire for glory and power, and his third desperate attempt was based solely on pride. He covered every base and still lost the game.

Samson and Delilah

So far, in every Biblical story we've examined, Satan failed. Now let's examine one where he succeeded. We have already discussed how God called, equipped, trained, and commissioned Samson; now let's stretch our imagination a little and look at the overall strategy Satan used to bring him down.

As he usually does, Satan started the fight with entry-level warfare. First, he sent a lion charging at Samson (see Judges 14:5-6). Samson may have felt like running, but instead he stood his ground and destroyed the lion with his bare hands. Satan lost the first round, but he was just getting warmed up. After seeing Samson's incredible display of supernatural strength, Satan realized that he would have to change his game plan.

He decided his best strategy was to match wits with his opponent at the gaming table. If he could get Samson to put all of his cards on the table, he believed he could win. One by one, he dealt each card. Play by play, Samson matched each bet and called every hand. Satan lost each time but as the card shark carefully watched his powerful opponent, he noticed that

Samson was a loner. His gift made him overly confident. After so many victories, he thought he couldn't lose. Another weakness Satan observed was that Samson was a man easily moved by passion. But above all, he saw that Samson never learned from his mistakes.

As they played the game, Samson told a riddle to his friends but he kept the answer to himself. His wife nagged him incessantly until he confided in her. That was a mistake! She betrayed his confidence and revealed his secret but God was faithful. He helped Samson pay his debt.

His passion drove him into a harlot's bed. His enemies lay in wait all around the city, waiting for morning light. But God intervened. Samson rose at midnight and walked off with the city's gates. His strength never abated. He seemed invincible.

The devil shuffled the deck and dealt one more hand, but this time the wily gambler dealt Samson one off the bottom. While quietly dealing Samson the Joker he slipped the Queen of Hearts into his pocket. Her name was Delilah. She was a lot like Samson's first wife. She nagged a lot but she was so pretty he never noticed.

> [Delilah] said unto him [Sampson], How canst thou say, I love thee, when thine heart is not with me? Thou hast mocked me these three times, and hast not told me wherein thy great strength lieth. And it came to pass, when she pressed him daily with her words, and urged him, so that his soul was vexed unto death; That he told her all his heart, and said unto her. There hath not come a razor upon mine head; for *I have been a Nazarite unto God from my mother's womb:* if I be shaven, then my strength will go from me, and I shall become weak, and be like any other man.
>
> -Judges 16:15-17, italics mine

THE MASTER'S VOICE

Satan realized that Samson's strength was in his covenant. All the devil had to do was get him to break his covenant, and then he would win.

> And she [Delilah] made him [Sampson] sleep upon her knees; and she called for a man, and she caused him to shave off the seven locks of his head; and she began to afflict him, and his strength went from him. And she said, The Philistines be upon thee, Samson. And he awoke out of his sleep, and said, I will go out as at other times before, and shake myself.
> -Judges 16:19-20

Delilah means *feeble*. God is not the only one who uses that which is feeble to defeat those who are strong. The flesh is weak. Don't let it take you down.

Samson's smug, self-confidence prevented him from asking God for wisdom. Before matching wits with the devil, we need to ask God for wisdom. We need all we can get.

> Behold, I send you forth as sheep in the midst of wolves: be ye therefore wise as serpents, and harmless as doves.
> -Matthew 10:16

Chapter Sixteen
Clean Vessels and Pure Words

> Depart ye, depart ye, go ye out from thence, touch no unclean thing; go ye out of the midst of her; be ye clean, that bear the vessels of the Lord.
> -Isaiah 52:11

What hidden motive lies in the heart of a prophet who speaks from his own heart instead of speaking through the inspiration of the Holy Spirit? To answer this question, let's use our imagination and examine a brief, somewhat fictitious rendering of a biblical story of one who did just that – Zedekiah (see 2 Chronicles 18:1-34).

Exhibitionism

There was a festive atmosphere in Ahab's palace. A visiting dignitary was being entertained. He was no stranger, to be sure. His son had married Athaliah, the king's daughter, but this time there was something special about his visit. The king had called for the prophets to assemble in the court tomorrow. He was contemplating going to war.

They were excited. Opportunities didn't come around like this every day. Zedekiah feverishly worked on into the night. He could hear the noise from the royal party through his shop's wall. He knew the wine would flow freely until the party was over. The incessant beat of the drums meant a steady parade of pretty girls were twirling and dancing before the kings. The drums finally quieted just as he slipped into bed. It was a little after two o'clock.

THE MASTER'S VOICE

He smiled sleepily as he thought about the impression he would make tomorrow. His iron horns were nearly ready. All they needed now was a good polishing. He would have time for that in the morning. He knew the meeting wouldn't be until late in the afternoon – the king would have to have time to recover from his hangover. His thoughts trailed off as he drifted to sleep.

The cock's incessant crowing annoyed him as he stirred, shielding his eyes from the bright glare of the morning sun filtering through his window lattice; nevertheless, he was glad to be awake. He dressed quickly, thinking about all the things he still had to do before getting ready for the meeting. He smiled again as he picked up the horns he had nearly completed the night before. He turned them over in his hands and admired the smooth curve of the horns. He would be the star of the show. The king would be impressed, he knew. Ahab liked that sort of thing. He wasn't so sure about the visiting monarch Jehoshaphat, though. He would just have to wait and see.

That afternoon, the prophets excitedly talked among themselves as they gathered in the court, waiting for the king's arrival. All four hundred were dressed to kill. Zedekiah was careful not to get his white suit stained as he carefully maneuvered his way to the front.

"Zedekiah, what are you going to tell him?" a voice shouted from the crowd as he settled into his place. "What do you *think* I'm going to say? He's going to *win*, isn't he?" Zedekiah scornfully replied. They should know by now, he thought, you don't tell a *king* he's going to *lose*!

A hush fell on the crowd as the king's drummer hit a continuous roll to bring them to attention. The kings had arrived. And what a sight they were. Their royal robes and jewel studded, golden crowns were breathtaking. The prophets bowed deeply as the kings settled upon their thrones. They anxiously waited for their invitation to speak. It wasn't long in coming.

"Shall we go to Ramoth-Gilead to battle, or shall I forbear?" Ahab loudly asked. The reply was thunderous! "Go up; for God will deliver it into the king's hand." They were unanimous.

After the clamor died down, the king turned to Zedekiah and asked, "Zedekiah, what has god shown you?" Zedekiah breathlessly stepped forward, unwrapping his handiwork as he went. Placing the glittering horns against his forehead, he twisted and turned as he prophesied. "Thus saith the Lord, With these you shall push Syria until they are consumed."

One can see from this brief story that everything Zedekiah said and did was motivated by the desire for honor. There's nothing wrong in wanting honor. It is a natural desire common to all. What is important is who we receive honor from. Jesus asked, "How can you believe, who receive honor from one another, and do not seek the honor that *comes* from the only God?" (John 5:44, NKJ) Then he said, "If any man serve me, him will my father honor" (John 12:26b).

One Voice Among Many

Although all of Baal's prophets were in agreement, there was one dissenting voice that day – Micaiah's. What difference does one dissenting voice among four hundred make? In Ahab's case, the difference between life and death. He died in the ensuing battle.

THE MASTER'S VOICE

Ahab heard what he wanted to hear. Jehoshaphat wasn't so sure, but he foolishly went along with the crowd. Hanging out with the wrong crowd nearly cost him his life. Although God mercifully spared him and got him out of his predicament, he was in hot water when he got back home. God sent a seer to reprove him. His mood was dark; his words were pungent and to the point.

> And Jehu the son of Hanani the seer went out to meet him, and said to king Jehoshaphat, Shouldest thou help the ungodly, and love them that hate the Lord? Therefore is wrath upon thee from before the Lord.
>
> 2 Chronicles 19:2

Zedekiah and his fellow prophets got Ahab killed and put Jehoshaphat in mortal danger. They ministered out of their own heart, and their hearts were deceived. They were incapable of ministering a pure word because their vessels were dirty. You can't serve clean milk from a dirty glass. Or, as one proverb says, "Whatever is in the well will come up in the bucket."

Deceived Prophets

God uses deceived prophets to deceive people who want to be deceived.

> Therefore speak unto them, and say unto them, Thus saith the Lord God; Every man of the house of Israel that sets up his idols in his heart, and puts the stumbling block of his iniquity before his face, and comes to the prophet; I the Lord will answer him that cometh according to the multitude of his idols... And if the prophet be

> deceived when he hath spoken a thing, I the Lord have deceived that prophet, and I will stretch out my hand upon him, and will destroy him from the midst of my people Israel. And they shall bear the punishment of their iniquity: the punishment of the prophet shall be even as the punishment of him that seeketh unto him.
> -Ezekiel 14:4,9-10

When God's prophets allow such uncleanness as jealousy, envy, bitterness, anger, lust, greed, or pride to contaminate their hearts, their ministry will be tainted. James said the wisdom from above is without hypocrisy.

> But if ye have bitter envying and strife in your hearts, glory not, and lie not against the truth. This wisdom descends not from above, but is earthly, sensual, devilish. For where envying and strife is, there is confusion and every evil work. But the wisdom that is from above is first pure, then peaceable, gentle, and easy to be entreated, full of mercy and good fruits, without partiality, and without hypocrisy.
> -James 3:14-17

Deceived ministers will minister deception. This is even true where doctrine is involved. Teachers teach what they believe, whether it's right or wrong. Likewise, it's possible for incorrect doctrine to be reflected in the prophecies of prophets who believe incorrectly. That's one reason it's so important for prophets to *know* the word.

Prophets who minister out of hurt will minister hurtful things. Bitter people are hard people. John said hatred blinds eyes. Ministers who desire man's honor will say and do whatever it takes to obtain their honor. Prophets who want to be true prophets have no other choice – they must follow straight paths of peace.

> And make straight paths for your feet, lest that which is lame be turned out of the way; but let it rather be healed. Follow peace with all men, and holiness, without which no man shall see the Lord: Looking diligently lest any man fail of the grace of God; lest any root of bitterness springing up trouble you, and thereby many be defiled.
> -Hebrews 12:13-15

Pure prophets minister pure words. God's true prophets minister truth. Sooner or later, defiled ministers defile those whom they minister to. It doesn't matter whether they are apostles, prophets, pastors, or teachers, the results are the same. They can't help themselves. You can't pick good fruit from a corrupt tree. Whatever grows there, grows naturally.

> If a man therefore purge himself from these, he shall be a vessel unto honor, sanctified, and meet for the master's use, and prepared unto every good work.
> -2 Timothy 2:21

CHAPTER SEVENTEEN
Healing and Deliverance

> How God anointed Jesus of Nazareth with the Holy Ghost and with power: who went about doing good, and healing all that were oppressed of the devil; for God was with him.
>
> -Acts 10:38

I seldom pass up an opportunity to witness for the Lord. Once, while working on a kitchen appliance in a home somewhere in the Midwest, I was engaged in a polite conversation with the homeowner. Somehow, the conversation turned to the subject of religion. I asked the man if he was a minister. He said, "Oh, no! Paul said that a bishop must have his children in subjection. I only have one child, so I'm not qualified." I listened in stunned silence. "Talk about legalistic," I thought, "this man is so narrow-minded he could look through a keyhole with both eyes at once!"

Our conversation then drifted over to divine healing. "God doesn't heal anymore," the man stated emphatically, "The Greek verb tenses are exact! Every time the Bible mentions divine healing, the tenses always indicate that healing is a thing of the past. It's not for today!"

I paused for a moment before answering. "I don't know much about the Greek tenses," I replied, "but I used to have severe headaches and a man prayed for me one night in Jena, Louisiana and I've never had one since." It was his turn to be silent.

I've often wondered how anyone can believe that God will one day raise the dead – and raise them from dust and ashes, at that – and not believe that healing is for today. Did God leave and go on vacation?

Revelation Gifts

I've checked out the verb tenses since our conversation that day, and that man was completely wrong. The Greek tenses used in the Bible definitely show that God still heals. Not only does He heal, He even goes out of His way to help us believe for our healing. That's one of the extra benefits of using a word of knowledge when ministering prophetically.

When a stranger accurately reveals your infirmities, it's not hard to believe that the same God who showed him your sickness will heal you as well. The effects of the gifts of miracles and healing are greatly enhanced by the gifts of revelation (wisdom, knowledge and discerning of spirits). While Paul was preaching in Lystra, he discerned a man's faith. He responded in like kind, releasing instant, resurrection power.

> And there sat a certain man at Lystra, impotent in his feet, being a cripple from his mother's womb, who never had walked: The same heard Paul speak: who steadfastly beholding him, and perceiving that he had faith to be healed, Said with a loud voice, Stand upright on thy feet. And he leaped and walked.
>
> -Acts 14:8-10

Someone once said the best spiritual gift was whichever one they needed at the moment. That's certainly true when we are sick. When I've got the flu, I'm not really interested in much of anything except getting rid of it. I thank God that He's not on vacation.

In fact, He's still quite active in the lives of His children today. He still reveals, and He still heals, if we only believe.

> Bless the LORD, O my soul,
> And forget not all His benefits:
> Who forgives all your iniquities,
> Who heals all your diseases
> -Psalm 103:2-3 NKJ

Deliverance Today

Besides physical healing, deliverance is also needed today. God isn't the only one who's not on vacation. The devil hasn't quit either. Isaiah said one of the purposes of the Holy Spirit's anointing was, "to proclaim liberty to the captives, and the opening of the prison to them that are bound" (Isaiah 61:1).

One prime example of the need for deliverance is Christians who suffer from depression, or as Isaiah called it, "the spirit of heaviness" (Isaiah 61:3). Many of these people can be helped when Jesus' command to cast out demons is taken seriously.

> As ye go, preach, saying, The kingdom of heaven is at hand. Heal the sick, cleanse the lepers, raise the dead, cast out devils: freely ye have received, freely give.
> -Matthew 10:7-8

The Gospel has been declared as The Good News. However, it's not good news to a person who is suffering from chronic depression to tell them that God doesn't deliver anyone anymore. Instead, Jesus ordered His ministers to include deliverance as part of the Gospel message. (This is not to imply that *all* depression is demonic in origin. Deficiencies in diet and chemical imbalances may also cause depression.)

The gift of discerning of spirits is the primary tool for use in exorcism. To discern means to mentally ascertain. Paul said, "so fight I, not as one that beats the air" (1 Corinthians 9:26b). We cannot be effective in battling demons without discerning their presence. We can't just shadow box and beat against the air. We have to know what we are dealing with.

God can reveal a demon's presence and identity to you several different ways. He may *tell* you one is there, or you may simply *feel* the demon's presence. He may *show* you a vision of its form, or you may recognize it from one or more of its manifestations. Either way, a demon cannot remain hidden in the shadows when God is shining light on it.

Discernment, along with the gift of miracles, allows us to see into the darkness of Satan's kingdom and liberate God's kids.

> And John answered him, saying, Master, we saw one casting out devils in thy name, and he followeth not us: and we forbad him, because he followeth not us. But Jesus said, Forbid him not: for there is no man which shall do a miracle in my name, that can lightly speak evil of me.
> -Mark 9:38-39

One of the surest signs that God is around is the devil being on the run. Jesus said, "if I with the finger of God cast out devils, *no doubt* the kingdom of God is come upon you" (Luke 11:20, italics mine).

When Jesus sent the seventy out to minister, He told them to heal the sick and preach the Kingdom of God. When they returned they were jubilant because they discovered that when they preached the

Kingdom, they saw miracles happen, including demons fleeing at their command. Jesus responded not only by confirming their authority over demons, but also by assuring them of divine protection when they were confronting them.

> Behold, I give unto you power to tread on serpents and scorpions, and over all the power of the enemy: and nothing shall by any means hurt you.
> -Luke 10:19

There is one thing about the deliverance ministry that cannot be over emphasized–whoever is ministering should be careful not to offend. Most exorcisms should be performed privately. There is nothing to be gained by embarrassing people when publicly revealing their private lives before the whole world. They need deliverance not humiliation (see 1 Corinthians 10:32; 2 Corinthians 6:3). Use wisdom, and remember the golden rule: minister to them as you would want to be ministered to yourself.

Objections Overruled

Some deliverance ministers disagree with that advice, claiming that Jesus always cast out demons publicly. Although there *are* several scriptural examples of public exorcisms, with the exception of those involving physical healing, they are usually confrontational in nature, not voluntary. When Jesus was challenged by a demon, He invariably rebuked it and cast it out, even if the encounter was in public. Otherwise, He was more discreet.

The Bible says that as Jesus traveled around the country ministering, He was accompanied by the twelve disciples along with, "certain women, which had been healed of evil spirits and infirmities, [including] Mary called Magdalene, out of whom went seven devils" (Luke 8:2). *When* He ministered to these women (some of whom were prostitutes, like Mary Magdalene), no one knows for sure. Christ did not permit us to watch. Instead, the Bible gives us the story after the fact.

While on this subject, another fact worth mentioning is this: many people do not believe that Christians *can* have demons. They reason that if they have the spirit of Christ, and are filled with the Holy Spirit, then demons cannot dwell in them. They do admit, however, that Christians can be *oppressed* by demons. So, rather than having to deal with this issue, when ministering deliverance simply use commands similar to "I command this spirit to *leave*." Whether it is oppressing them from the inside or outside is immaterial. If it is inside, it has to come out to leave. If it is not, so much the better; either way, the demon is gone and its victim is free.

Praying in tongues is another way of privately ministering deliverance, even in a public setting. No one besides God (and possibly the one you are ministering to) knows what you are praying for. In fact, praying in tongues is one of the most effective tools that God has provided for this purpose. Both physical and emotional healing, as well as deliverance, can be accomplished this way. We are not always aware of everything a person needs, but God is, and "makes intercession for the saints according to the will of God" (Romans 8:27). It can't get any easier than that!

A Valid Ministry

The Bible declares that deliverance reveals the power of God's Kingdom. Likewise, healing provides a window into His heart, revealing His compassion and mercy. On the other hand, prophecy reveals the hidden things of a sinner's heart, causing him to fall on his knees and confess that God's Spirit is truly in the one being used of God to prophesy. There are so many wonderful and positive results from true, supernatural, prophetic ministry that all we need is more of it. It reveals His marvelous presence in ways that no other ministry can.

> A gift is as a precious stone in the eyes of him that hath it: whithersoever it turns, it prospers.
> -Proverbs 17:8

THE MASTER'S VOICE

CHAPTER EIGHTEEN
Unusual Manifestations

> I have also spoken by the prophets, and I have multiplied visions, *and used similitudes*, by the ministry of the prophets.
> -Hosea 12:10, italics mine

Prophets sometimes use similitudes to indicate what God is saying to the people. These similitudes are living illustrations used to make a particular point. If we saw a prophet do some of the things today that Israel's prophets did in Old Testament times, we'd have him locked up! Isaiah would be arrested for indecent exposure. He walked around "naked and barefoot three years for a sign and wonder upon Egypt and upon Ethiopia" (Isaiah 20:3). Jeremiah may have escaped arrest, but he wouldn't have earned much respect either. God had him make wooden yokes and wear them around his neck to illustrate what the Israelites would look like after Nebuchadnezzar got through with them (see Jeremiah 27:1-2).

But Ezekiel would almost certainly be carted off to the asylum! He acted like a kid playing with toy soldiers. God told him to take a clay tile "and lay siege against it, and build a fort against it, and cast a mount against it; set the camp also against it, and set battering rams against it round about" (Ezekiel 4:2). And that was just the beginning. Next, Ezekiel took an iron pan to illustrate the city's walls and laid beside it on his left side, as if he was paralyzed. He did this for three hundred and ninety days, then he turned over and laid on his right side for another forty days.

During all this time, he was living on a starvation diet and cooking his food with cow's dung.

Similitudes Today

These are just three examples out of dozens recorded in the Old Testament. You might be thinking, "Yes, but that was the *Old* Testament. They operated different back then." *Wrong!* Here is one right out of the New Testament.

> And as we tarried there many days, there came down from Judaea a certain prophet, named Agabus. And when he was come unto us, he took Paul's girdle, and bound his own hands and feet, and said, Thus saith the Holy Ghost, So shall the Jews at Jerusalem bind the man that owns this girdle, and shall deliver him into the hands of the Gentiles.
>
> -Acts 21:10-11

God would probably show His people more things today if His prophets would yield to Him. There seems to be a restoration of this aspect of the prophetic ministry in process now. God is again raising up a few Agabuses.

Special Miracles

God is currently restoring special miracles in Church.

> And God wrought *special miracles* by the hands of Paul: So that from his body were brought unto the sick handkerchiefs or aprons, and the diseases departed from them, and the evil spirits went out of them.
> -Acts 19:11-12, italics mine

Special miracles are signs and wonders for which there is no scriptural precedence. Besides healing and delivering people who were touched by Paul's handkerchiefs, God also did some special miracles through Peter, only He used Peter's shadow instead of his handkerchiefs.

> Insomuch that they brought forth the sick into the streets, and laid them on beds and couches, that at the least the shadow of Peter passing by might overshadow some of them.
> -Acts 5:15

Prayer cloths are quite common now, but there is nothing special about them. Since Paul's day, we've had scriptural precedence for them. Even if God starts using someone's shadow to heal, it's still nothing new. We need something special, and it is only special if it's never been done before! Also, we shouldn't be too amazed if we see God do something special in which no one gets healed. Peter walking on the water was certainly special, but no one received any healing or deliverance from his supernatural demonstration.

Peter's amazing feat of walking on water pales in comparison to another special miracle found in Scripture. After Phillip the evangelist left Samaria, an angel sent him into the desert to witness to a lone traveler. After he completed his mission, instead of walking on to the next town, "the Spirit of the Lord caught away Philip, that the eunuch saw him no more... But Philip was found at Azotus" (Acts 8:39-40).

The Holy Spirit's manifestations are many and varied. For instance, the Bible reveals at least three different methods used by Jesus to heal the blind (see Matthew 20:34; Mark 8:23; John 9:6-7). He never raised the dead the same way twice. When He created the universe, He seems to have delighted in diversity. Even the stars differ one from another (see 1 Corinthians 15:41).

Instead of diversity, people love security. Although we may say, "Variety is the spice of life," in reality, we are creatures of habit. Although variety attracts us, it also threatens us (especially religious variety). It makes us nervous when we encounter something supernatural for the first time. Hopefully, God will expand our minds and enlarge our expectations as we get nearer to the end. I'm looking forward to it.

> Now there are *diversities* of gifts, but the same Spirit. And there are *differences* of administrations, but the same Lord. And there are *diversities* of operations, but it is the same God which worketh all in all. But the manifestation of the Spirit is given to every man to profit withal.
> -1 Corinthians 12:4-7, italics mine

Slain in the Spirit

Although there is still some controversy, there is one sign and wonder, which has become so common that it's hardly a wonder anymore. I'm referring to being "slain in the Spirit." There are several scriptural examples of this manifestation, found in both the Old and New Testaments.

One of the first men to encounter this strange phenomenon was King Saul. When David was running from Saul, things got so hot for him that he fled to where Samuel was staying. The king found out where he was camped and sent messengers to apprehend him, but when his men got around Samuel, they started prophesying and went home. After three failed attempts, Saul decided to go and see for himself just what was going on. When he arrived at Samuel's he did the same as the others, except for one thing; he was slain in the spirit all night long.

> And he stripped off his clothes also, and prophesied before Samuel in like manner, and lay down naked all that day and all that night. Wherefore they say, Is Saul also among the prophets?
> -1 Samuel 19:24

What was he saying when he prophesied? He wasn't *saying* anything. He was simply performing a similitude, *showing* himself that he was totally in the flesh. God has a sense of humor.

Saul's son Jonathan experienced the same phenomenon, except instead of him being slain in the spirit, his enemies were. In one of the most amazing victories in the Old Testament, God caused twenty of Jonathan's enemies to fall down in front of him where all he had to do was watch his armor bearer slay them.

> And the men of the garrison answered Jonathan and his armorbearer, and said, Come up to us, and we will shew you a thing. And Jonathan said unto his armorbearer, Come up after me: for the Lord hath delivered them into the hand of Israel. And Jonathan climbed up upon his hands and upon his feet, and his armorbearer after him: and they

> fell before Jonathan; and his armorbearer slew after him.
>
> -1 Samuel 14:12-13

Daniel was slain in the Spirit after an angel visited him. In fact, the Spirit was so strong upon him that he had trouble staying conscious in the angel's presence (see Daniel 8:17-18, 27). In the New Testament, the night before Jesus' crucifixion a mixed band of ruffians fell backward in the garden when Jesus called out the words, "I am He" to them.

> As soon then as [Jesus] had said unto them, I am he, they went backward, and fell to the ground.
>
> -John 18:6

The most famous occurrence of anyone being slain in the Spirit is also found in the New Testament. When Peter confronted Ananias and Sapphira about lying to the Holy Ghost, they were immediately *slain* in the Spirit. However, this time, they didn't get back up because they died.

Counterfeit Signs

Agabus used Paul's girdle to illustrate his point. Zedekiah's prop was a set of iron horns. What is the difference? Both men added a visual dimension to the message being delivered, enhancing its effect and making it that much more effective.

The answer lies not in what was used, or even what action was taken, but in *why* a prop was used in the first place. What was its purpose? Agabus used Paul's girdle because the Holy Spirit instructed him to. God wanted to emphasize His point. Zedekiah used iron horns because he was motivated by a spirit of exhibitionism. He wanted to show off.

Solomon said, "It is not good to eat much honey: so for men to search their own glory is not glory" (Proverbs 25:27). Zedekiah didn't glorify himself as he sought to do, instead he made himself a fool. He prophesied through the inspiration of a spirit of *divination*, and his actions were inspired by a spirit of *exhibitionism*.

In Acts, Luke writes that when he and Paul were ministering in Macedonia, they were met by a damsel "possessed with a spirit of divination... The same followed Paul and us, and cried, saying, These men are the servants of the most high God, which shew unto us the way of salvation" (Acts 16:16-17). She did this for several days before Paul grew tired of her nonsense and cast the demon out of her. Like Zedekiah, she was motivated by a spirit of exhibitionism to seek glory for herself. Jesus said:

> *He that speaketh of himself seeketh his own glory*: but he that seeketh his glory that sent him, the same is true, and no unrighteousness is in him.
> -John 7:18, italics mine

"Of himself" doesn't mean *about* himself, although that can be part of counterfeit ministry; it means he is speaking of his own initiative. What he is saying is coming out of his own heart instead of God's. Like the damsel mentioned above, she wasn't talking *about* herself – she was speaking *for* herself – from her own heart! She was attempting to glorify herself by identifying herself with those much greater than herself – the apostles.

In contrast, Jesus said, "I do nothing of myself" (John 8:28), meaning the source of all His actions were from the Father's initiative. So, it's not *what* we do that matters as much as *why* we do what we do.

This is true whether we are using props and skits to illustrate a point, dancing in front of the congregation, falling down by being slain in the spirit, or yielding to unusual manifestations. The motivation for our actions is important, not the actions themselves. God judges the heart.

Why not just stick with speaking the word and discard all the rest? Because only things of real value are worth counterfeiting. If they were not valuable, God wouldn't have used them in the first place, and Satan wouldn't be working so hard to mint counterfeit copies. When we, out of fear of getting off base, quit playing altogether, we forfeit the game and lose.

Fear of getting out of bounds and making mistakes has robbed the Church. Many churches won't even allow their members to speak in tongues, much less prophesy. The idea is, "If we don't allow it, we don't have to deal with it." The truth is, in rejecting the Holy Spirit's manifestations, they have rejected God and denied His Word.

He said *covet* to prophesy, not *avoid* prophecy. He also said *judge* prophets and prophecy, not *forbid* them. And, in an attempt to ward off Satan's attack against the gifts, He even had Paul warn the Church to "forbid not to speak with tongues" (1 Corinthians 14:39). We have several hundred years of tradition and error to reverse before we can fully embrace all that God has provided for us. He doesn't change. He's still on the throne. His provisions are only limited when we refuse to obey.

God also bearing them witness, both with signs and wonders, and with divers miracles, and gifts of the Holy Ghost, *according to his own will.*
-Hebrews 2:4, italics mine

THE MASTER'S VOICE

CHAPTER NINETEEN
Questions and Answers

> And it came to pass, that after three days they found him in the temple, sitting in the midst of the doctors, both hearing them, and asking them questions.
>
> -Luke 2:46

To complete this discussion on prophets and personal prophecy, I'll address certain questions which regularly come up when I teach prophetic seminars. For ease of writing, I will only use the male gender, but the gift of prophecy is given equally to men and women (or boys and girls) alike.

Some of these questions have been thoroughly discussed and answered in previous chapters of this book, but are reintroduced here for additional clarification.

1. What is the difference between the gift of prophecy, and the gift of the word of wisdom and the word of knowledge?

All three are manifestations of the Holy Spirit, but they each operate differently. The *gift of prophecy* provides a direct, divine oracle from God. What God says, the prophet repeats. The prophet speaks the prophecy "word for word." The gifts of wisdom and knowledge operate differently. The *gift of wisdom* is the *ability* to obtain knowledge and use it correctly, while *knowledge* is a certain perception of things that exist. Although different prophets minister differently, most *public* prophecy is delivered "word for word," but most *personal* prophecy is a mixture of all three gifts. In fact, during personal ministry, any of the nine gifts may be used, singularly, or in combination with each other.

2. What is meant by the terms, public prophecy and personal prophecy?

Public (or *congregational*) prophecy is a message delivered to the whole congregation. *Personal* prophecy is a message given to an individual. *Personal* prophecy can also include additional ministry, such as divine healing and deliverance.

3. First Corinthians 14:32 says, "the spirits of the prophets are subject to the prophets." Explain what that Scripture means.

The "spirit of the prophet" is the prophet's anointing. When a prophet is prophesying, he is fully in control. He can choose to speak, or not to speak. God doesn't *take over* and make him say or do things without his cooperation and participation. This is also true for those who do not actually hold the office of a prophet, but who, nevertheless, have the gift of prophecy and minister prophetically.

Although the spirit is under the prophet's control, the actual content of the prophecy is not. In other words, he is not allowed to decide what he is going to say. If he speaks at all, it should be by the inspiration of the Holy Spirit.

The easiest way to illustrate this is to imagine the prophet's anointing as an envelope in which God uses to send His message. The letter inside the envelope is the prophecy, itself. The prophet is in control. He can choose to open the envelope and read the letter, or not to read it. If he decides to read it, he must read it as it is written. He isn't allowed to change what it says.

Most *public* prophecy is given this way. On the other hand, most (but not all) *personal* prophecy is actually ministered through the word of wisdom and the word of knowledge. Using these gifts, the prophet receives the revelation of the subject matter, and under the Holy Spirit's direction, works out the best wording and method to deliver the message.

4. Since a prophet isn't allowed to change the prophecy's content, why is he responsible to minister correction without hurting people's feelings?

There are several things to consider in answering this question. First, the *spirit* in which something is said is often as important as *what* is said. The tone of the speaker's voice can influence the way a message is received. Pausing during the delivery, or placing emphasis on certain parts of the message can change the way it is perceived by those who hear it.

Secondly, because the spirit of the prophet is subject to the prophet, before he delivers the message, he can usually choose how he is going to minister.

Seasoned prophets can activate the gift of prophecy, and speak verbatim, *or* use the gift of wisdom and under the Holy Spirit's direction, give the word in the way that it will do the most good. Remember, the *object* is to edify the people, not just to prophesy.

> Even so ye, forasmuch as ye are zealous of spiritual gifts, *seek that ye may excel to the edifying of the church.*
> -1 Corinthians 14:12, italics mine

5. Isn't it wrong to seek spiritual gifts? Aren't we, as some teach, supposed to, "seek the Giver, not the gifts"?

No, it is *not* wrong to seek for the gifts of the Spirit (see 1 Corinthians 12:31). Those who ignorantly teach, "seek the Giver, *not* the gifts," are actually teaching *contrary* to Scripture! The Bible commands us to seek the Giver *and* His gifts!

The truth is, when you seek God for spiritual gifts, you *are* seeking the giver. Spiritual gifts are "the manifestation of the Spirit." The more of His gifts you have, the more of His anointing you have. The two are inseparable. You can't manifest His Spirit if you don't have it! Paul plainly said, "covet earnestly the best gifts," and "brethren, covet to prophesy" (1 Corinthians 12:31, 14:39).

Those who teach contrary to Scripture may have good intentions, but their doctrine is wrong. God wants us to seek *both* Him *and* His gifts!

6. Didn't Paul say that love was better than the gifts? If we have love, then we don't need spiritual gifts, right?

This is another common misconception. What Paul actually said was, "But covet earnestly the best gifts: and yet shew I unto you a more excellent way" (1 Corinthians 12:31).

In this verse, and in the following chapter, Paul teaches that operating the gifts without love is unprofitable. He didn't say love was *better* than spiritual gifts. He said that loving people was a "more excellent way" of *obtaining* spiritual gifts. He knew that some people seek the gifts because they want to use them for their own purposes, as when Simon the sorcerer tried to get Peter to sell him the power to lay hands on people so they would receive the Holy Spirit. Selfish desire for fame and gain is not the right motive for coveting the gifts.

If you love people, and they are sick or sad and depressed, it is natural to want to alleviate their suffering. The Bible teaches that if we love someone, then we should endeavor to help them when they are in need (see 1 John 3:17:18; James 15:16).

If they need divine direction, and you don't have the gift of a word of wisdom, how can you give them what they need? If they are sick, and you don't have the gifts of healing, basically all you can do is take them to a doctor, and how is God glorified in that?

Love is the proper *motive* for *seeking* spiritual gifts – it isn't a *substitute* for them! After Paul wrote the chapter about love, and taught the proper use of the gifts, he concluded with "Wherefore, brethren, covet to prophesy, and forbid not to speak with tongues" (1 Corinthians 14:39).

7. Why do some ministers use the title "prophet," and some, who appear to be prophets, do not? Aren't they exalting themselves if they claim to be prophets?

Personally, I don't care for titles, but I don't censor those who choose to use them. I do, however, when asked about my ministry, answer that I minister in the office of a prophet, or that I minister prophetically. It isn't any more wrong for a prophet to call himself a prophet than it is for your pastor to call himself a pastor, or an evangelist to call himself and evangelist. There's no difference.

8. Sometimes, people who are attempting to minister are not real sure if what they are hearing is from God or not. Is this normal? What should they do to be sure?

It is perfectly normal to question what you hear, or see, or even feel, especially when you first start prophesying. Even Jeremiah had problems at times. God told him his uncle was going to offer to sell him some land. When his uncle showed up and made the offer, he said, "Then I knew that this was the word of the Lord" (Jeremiah 32:6-8). Gideon's faith was even weaker than that. God had to send him an angel, make a fleece wet, then dry, and then let him listen in on a dream and its interpretation before he was fully convinced that he could trust what he was hearing (see Judges 6:11-40, 7:1-15).

When you think you've received something for someone, if you are unsure, ask them if what you have is correct. For instance, if you're praying for someone and you are impressed that they have back trouble, ask them if their back has been bothering them. Through experience, you'll soon learn to know when it's God, and when it's not.

9. Given enough time, some prophets can prophesy to everyone in the room; yet some people can only minister to two or three. Why?

Most prophets can prophesy at will, sometimes to someone who isn't even present in the room. Saints who are not prophets, but minister through the gift of prophecy are usually more limited. If you are faithful to minister to those God gives you something for, He will advance you in due time. Just keep seeking Him for more.

10. Some prophets prophesy specific details about people's lives, including things like peoples' names, or specific dates of events that occurred in the past. Others prophesy in more vague and general terms. Why is there a difference?

There are several reasons. One is experience. The more experience a person receives, the more confident he becomes. This allows him to relax and perceive things of a more precise nature.

Another reason is some people have a *natural* ability to perceive things in the spiritual realm. When

God calls these people into His service, they quickly move into a deeper level of revelation than those who do not have the same natural sensitivity. You can think of it in this way: Musical talent is a gift, but all musicians aren't gifted alike. Some are much more skillful than others are.

11. What is the difference between a seer and a prophet?

Biblically, there isn't much difference. First Samuel 9:9 says: "He that is now called a prophet was before-time called a seer." As you can see, in Scripture, they appear to be two different names for the same office.

The actual difference is not in what they do but in how they receive their information. Although visions are common to both prophets and seers, a seer's primary revelation comes through visions while prophets receive their revelation primarily through hearing and intuition.

Fortunetellers and psychics are seldom called prophets but are usually referred to as *seers*, regardless of how they receive revelation knowledge.

12. What is the difference between a psychic and a prophet? Also, is there a difference in what they do?

Psychics, mediums, fortunetellers, palm readers, soothsayers, astrologers, sorcerers, witches and warlocks are all spiritual counterfeits. (I will use the generic term *"psychic"* to represent them all, but they have many different titles.) Since they're demonic counterfeits of true apostles and prophets, obviously, there are certain similarities in what God's ministers and psychics do.

The main difference between prophets and psychics is that prophets glorify God, while psychics attempt to glorify themselves. Prophets operate by the *Holy Spirit* (the *Spirit of Truth*; see John 16:13), but psychics operate by demons called *familiar spirits* or *spirit guides* (*lying spirits*, such as divination and exhibitionism). Prophets freely prophesy the oracles of God and psychics give readings for money. (That's *one* way you can judge prophets, by whether they prostitute the gifts or not [see Chapter Nine].)

There are many similarities in what psychics and prophets minister but one easily recognized difference is this: prophets attribute God's blessings to God (as everyone should), but psychics usually call His blessings good luck or good fortune.

God *encourages* people to go to His prophets and inquire of Him through them. He also exhorts people to *believe* His prophets. But, He *forbids* them going to His competitors, the psychics (see 2 Chronicles 20:20; 2 Kings 1:2-4; Deuteronomy 18:9-15). Those who do so provoke Him to jealousy and invite deception and trouble into their lives.

13. Can a prophet choose what subject he is going to address when he ministers to someone?

To a very great extent, yes. A prophet's viewpoint determines much of what he sees and hears. That's the reason a pessimistic prophet, or a prophet of doom as they are often called, always sees bad things coming. He sees what he's looking for.

The prophet should keep an open mind. We don't want to fall into the snare of crying, "peace, peace; when there is no peace" (Jeremiah 6:14), because occasionally, bad things *are* on the agenda. The prophet can and should look for whatever is coming, regardless of whether it is good or bad.

Pessimistic and paranoid prophets, who only see death and destruction coming upon everyone and everything, should examine their hearts for impurities, such as offenses, which are influencing their spiritual sight. God is not an ogre trying to *get* people; He's a loving Father trying to help and save them.

A prophet can search the Spirit in many different ways, about many different things. He can search for specific details about specific subjects, including *time*. There is no guarantee that God is going to reveal anything to him on the subject he is inquiring about, but quite often, He does. The following Scripture illustrates this point.

> Of which salvation the prophets have enquired [of God] and searched [the Spirit] diligently, who prophesied of the grace that should come unto you: *Searching what, or what manner of time* the Spirit of Christ which was in them did signify, when it testified beforehand the sufferings of Christ, and the glory that should follow.
> -1 Peter 1:10-11, italics mine

14. If a pastor refuses to give his people permission to prophesy in church, should they go ahead and prophesy anyway?

No, they should *not!* The Bible says, "Obey them that have the rule over you, and submit yourselves" (Hebrews 13:17). You cannot disobey the leaders the Holy Spirit has placed over you and still obey God at the same time. God and His word are always in harmony.

Of course, there are exceptions to almost every rule. For example, Peter and John disobeyed the magistrates who forbade them to preach in Jesus' name and went ahead and ministered anyway. *But, they had a direct command from an angel to do so, so their case was an exception.* They were not ministering in rebellion, they were obeying the higher authority (see Acts 5:18-29 and Romans 13:1). Usually, that's not the case.

If your pastor will not allow you to minister in his church, you should join or start a small group where spiritual gifts are welcomed. Also pray for God to open the pastor's heart to embrace the manifestations of the Spirit. If no other options are available, ask God for permission to change churches.

15. I've heard that only men of equal or greater rank can correct someone. For instance, only an apostle can rebuke an apostle, but an apostle can rebuke a prophet, pastor or teacher. Is that true?

No, it isn't! Balaam was rebuked by his donkey. I don't think a donkey is equal in rank to a prophet – not most prophets anyway (see 2 Peter 2:15-16). *Pride* is the root of that error. If a person is humble, he can receive correction from anyone, even a child. God will use whomever, or in the case of the donkey, whatever He has available.

In the times of the kings of Israel, the prophets were subject to the kings. Whenever a king did wrong, God would send a prophet to rebuke him. That didn't make the prophet equal to the king. It's the word of God which does the correcting and rebuking, not the vessel God uses. His word is above everyone and everything.

16. Some teachers teach the best way to judge a personal prophecy is to "put it on the shelf, and wait and see if it comes to pass." Is that wise?

No, it isn't. Jesus said His word is a seed (see Luke 8:11). If someone gives you a package of watermelon seeds and you put them on a shelf to see if they are fertile or not, you'll have to wait an awfully long time before you get to eat watermelons. The same holds true for prophetic promises. Paul said to meditate upon your prophecies and give yourself wholly to them (see 1 Timothy 4:15).

You *plant* God's word in your heart, *water* it with prayer and meditation, *fertilize* it with personal sacrifices, and *reap* the promised provisions with joy. Personal prophecies placed on the shelf of forgetfulness never produce anything but disappointments.

17. Explain the difference between Scripture and personal prophecy. Is a personal prophecy, in any way, equal to Scripture?

This question is like asking if apples and oranges are the same thing. The answer is both yes *and* no. *Yes*, because both are fruits, and *no*, because they aren't the same kind of fruit. In the Greek language, Jesus and the Scriptures are called "logos." Conversely, a divinely inspired oracle or revelation is called a "rhema." All personal prophecy is rhema. Although logos and rhema are both God's word, they aren't exactly the same thing.

The logos is the established, unconditional word of God which is forever settled in heaven. Every prophecy in Scripture is Logos, and every Logos, in its time, *will* be fulfilled and come to pass.

A rhema, on the other hand, is that which God is *currently* speaking. Most personal prophecy is a rhema from God revealing His will under existing, stated or implied conditions. Because a rhema is conditional, it may or may not come to pass, depending upon our faith, obedience, etc. No authentic rhema ever contradicts the Logos.

18. Is it possible to have the author come and conduct a seminar on prophecy in our church?

THE MASTER'S VOICE

Yes! Your pastor can call or write me in order to schedule a meeting. You may want to give him a copy of this book. He will then be familiar with my approach to the prophetic ministry and have an idea of what to expect from the seminar. The address is in the front and on the back of this book.

Ira L. Milligan

SEVEN DIRECTIVES FOR MINISTERING THE GIFTS OF THE SPIRIT

1. Be gracious. Don't condemn or judge or be a busybody in other men's matters. Seek to edify the church: "But he that prophesies speaks unto men to edification, exhortation and comfort" (1 Corinthians 14:3; also see Romans 2:1-4; 1 Peter 4:15).

2. Don't quench the Spirit or change the order of the service. There is a proper time for ministry. Don't interrupt fellow ministers. Follow (obey) whoever is in charge.

3. Be willing to admit when you are wrong. No one is infallible. Learn from your mistakes. Don't defend them.

4. Keep public (congregational) prophecy short (one or two minutes, maximum).

5. *DO* minister under supervision. Be sure to minister in circumstances that allow others to judge your prophecy (record your words on tape when possible).

6. Never try to persuade or force others to obey or fulfill a prophetic word. To do so is witchcraft, or even sorcery! One who prophesies has no responsibility or authority to make anyone obey or fulfill a prophecy.

7. One who prophesies represents Christ. "The testimony of Jesus is the spirit of prophecy" (Revelation 19:10). Therefore speak the truth in love, for "Love worketh no ill to his neighbor" (Romans 13:10a).

ABOUT THE AUTHOR

Ira and Judy Milligan have served God since 1962. In 1986, they founded Servant Ministries, Inc. They travel and present such seminars as
- *Dreams and Their Interpretation*
- *Counseling and Inner Healing*
- *Personal Spiritual Warfare*
- *Prophets and Personal Prophecy*

Ira has taught classes on counseling as a guest lecturer at Oral Roberts University.

For information concerning seminars conducted in your church, contact Ira Milligan:

PO Box 1120
Tioga, LA 71477
www.Servant-Ministries.org

Other Books by Ira L. Milligan

- **Understanding the Dreams You Dream: Biblical Keys for Hearing God's Voice in the Night**
    God frequently talks through dreams. The Bible reveals that in the past, dreams were the most common way God talked to His people. Unlike the early Christians, today's believers often treat dreams like junk mail. In doing so, they often throw away the very answers they ask for when they pray for counsel and guidance.

Understanding the Dreams You Dream is written from a Christian perspective to help Christians understand the symbolic language of dreams. Deliberately written without technical jargon, this book can be easily understood and used by everyone. It is the only complete, one volume Christian reference book for interpreting dreams on the market today.

- **Understanding the Dreams You Dream Vol. II: Every Dreamer's Handbook**

    Have you ever dreamed that you won the lottery, but after waking couldn't remember the winning numbers? Frustrating! Equally frustrating is dreaming of looking for a specific house or room number, and although you wake up remembering the number, you have no idea what it means. Although numbers are rather common in dreams, most dream books just ignore them. This one doesn't.

    Ever dream of being attacked by fierce dragons? One women did, and discovered that her only effective defense was oranges! Even pieces of the oranges were sufficient to ward them off. What did the dragons and oranges represent? Every Dreamer's Handbook systematically teaches the language of dreams, providing answers to questions like these, explaining what dreams mean and why they mean what they mean.

- **Anatomy of a Scorpion: Illustrating The Wheel of Nature**

    "Behold, I give unto you power to tread on serpents and scorpions, and over all the power of the enemy" (Luke 10:19). Most Christians know that serpents symbolize demons, but very few know the truth and power that lies hidden in the scorpion's symbolism. The *Anatomy of a Scorpion* unveils this mystery and reveals it's practical application for every believer. A must for anyone interested in counseling and deliverance (price includes a counselor's aid, *The Wheel of Nature*).

- **Rightly Dividing the Word: Illustrating A Perfect Heart**

    One of God's favorite tactics to hide truth is to place it in plain sight, but disguise it as something other than what it is. Almost all spiritual truth is first clothed with a natural disguise. When we remove the natural covering, we find the naked truth. Like wheat, the natural husk must be removed from the grain before it is usable. An example of this is Moses' Law. The Law is spiritual, but it is clothed with various commandments and ordinances that hide its precious truths. These spiritual treasures are, "life unto those that find them, and health to all their flesh" (Proverbs 4:23). *Rightly Dividing the Word* carefully guides the serious Bible student step by step through the Scriptures to safely obtain these treasures.

- **The Hidden Power of Covenant: Releasing the Fullness of the Blessing of the Gospel of Jesus Christ**

    Paul wrote to the church in Rome and boldly declared, "And I am sure that, when I come unto you, I shall come in the fullness of the blessing of the gospel of Christ" (Romans

15:29). How could he be so sure? In fact, the New King James Version of the Bible translates Paul as saying, "I know that when I come to you, I shall come in the fullness of the blessing..." How could he be so confident? What did he know that made him so bold? And, besides that, just what is the fullness of the blessing of the Gospel, anyway? The answers are hidden deep in the mystery of covenant. This book probes and explores this mystery to reveal the surprising answers to these important questions.

www.ingramcontent.com/pod-product-compliance
Lightning Source LLC
Chambersburg PA
CBHW071205070526
44584CB00019B/2928